PEW EDITION

Edited by
David P. Polk

CHALICE
PRESS

ST. LOUIS, MISSOURI

Contents

A Word to Worshipers

You hold in your hands not just another supplement to a recent hymnal. This set of musical resources for the church's worship is a different type of collection. It specifically offers a gathering together of the best and often the freshest of songs that characterize contemporary Christian music.

Certainly no single volume can embrace the range of musical materials that a congregation will use in its contemporary or even "blended" service of worship. The aim here is to provide a reliable core from which the leadership team can draw, week after week, saving worship and music planners many long hours in their search and selection process.

Chalice Praise does serve as a companion resource to *Chalice Hymnal*. For that reason, no material in *Chalice Hymnal* is repeated here, and the full music edition contains an index of fifty-nine selections from that hymnal that expand the repertoire of this collection. But congregations using any hymnal will find in this volume a useful resource that will expand and enhance the musical breadth of their worshiping.

The flow of the songbook follows an order utilized in many contemporary worship services: gathering, centering, praying, responding, communing, departing. The communing section is for occasions of celebrating the eucharist. Use these groupings only as a starting point for incorporating these songs into your worship experiences.

The pew edition provides only the words, melody line, and guitar chords. The keyboard accompaniment is found in the full music edition, which also contains additional indexes (topical and musical keys). An introduction to an effective utilization of this resource in a broad range of congregational settings is found only in the full music edition.

Bringing this project to completion has truly been a labor of love. The screening and selection process depended on the contributions of a great team of core advisers who met with me over the period of more than a year. This songbook has been shaped by their wise and loving efforts. They are: Katrina Bright, Michael Carlson, Kathy Carson, Tim Carson, Martha Chenault, Cricket Harrison, Matthew Hunt, Wayne Kent, Rhonda McMahon, Andra Moran, Steve Reinhardt, and Steve Staicoff. In addition, Bill Thomas offered significant suggestions from afar. And Al Graves repeated his valuable work in setting all these pages on computer. A huge word of thanks is expressed to all of them, as to everyone who has had any hand in birthing this book.

David P. Polk, Editor

This Is the Day

WORDS and MUSIC: Bob Fitts

2   Come, Now Is the Time to Worship   *Phil. 2:9–11*

WORDS and MUSIC: Brian Doerksen

- ly   choose   You now.

come,   come,   come.

Psalm 95:6

Uyaimose

3

1. U - ya - i - mo - se,   ti - na - ma - te Mwa - ri;
2. Come all you peo - ple,   come and wor - ship Yah - weh;

u - ya - i - mo - se,   ti - na - ma - te Mwa - ri;
come all you peo - ple,   come and wor - ship Yah - weh;

u - ya - i - mo - se,   ti - na - ma - te Mwa - ri;
come all you peo - ple,   come and wor - ship Yah - weh;

u - ya - i - mo - se Zvi - no.
come now and wor - ship the Lord.

WORDS: Anon. (from Zimbabwe); paraphrase I-to Loh
MUSIC: Alexander Gondo

4   Bless the Lord, My Soul   *Psalm 103:1–5, 20–22*

Bless the Lord, my soul! Come be-fore him with sing - ing.

Praise the Lord, you an - gels and might-y ones on high!

Bless the Lord, my soul! Come be-fore him with danc - ing.

Praise the Lord, you heav - ens and stars up in the sky.

For - get not all his man - y bless - ings.

Re - mem - ber who re - deems your soul,

WORDS and MUSIC: Stephen Reinhardt

who fills your life with love and beau - ty,

who fills you up and makes you whole.

CODA

Praise the Lord, you hea - vens and stars up in the sky.

Praise him all cre - a - tion, and lift his name on high!

Psalm 103:1–5

[1] Bless the LORD, O my soul,
   and all that is within me,
   bless God's holy name.

[2] **Bless the LORD, O my soul,
   and do not forget all God's benefits—**

[3] who forgives all your iniquity,
   who heals all your diseases,

[4] who redeems your life from the Pit,
   who crowns you with steadfast love and mercy,

[5] **who satisfies you with good as long as you live
   so that your youth is renewed like the eagle's.**

5   Day and Night   *1 John 1:5–7, 2:8–11*

♩=128 *Boogie*

1. Shad-ows all a-round me, and star-less is my night.
2. Wait-in' for the sun - rise to come and fill the sky.

And now that love has found me I'll be
I can see the sun - shine when I

liv - in' in the light. Day and night shine a
look in - to your eyes.

bright, bright, light; bright be the light of God.

Day and night shine a bright, bright, light;

[1. E A/E] [2. E]

bright be the light of God. We are

WORDS and MUSIC: Andra Moran

The River Is Here

Revelation 22:1

1. Down the moun-tain the riv-er flows, and it
(2.) riv-er of God is teem-ing with life;

brings re-fresh-ing wher-ev-er it goes.
all who touch it can be re-vived, and

Through the val-leys and o-ver the fields the
those who lin-ger on this riv-er's shore will

riv-er is rush-ing and the riv-er is here. The
come back thirst-ing for more of the Lord. The

riv-er of God sets our feet a-danc-ing; the

riv-er of God fills our hearts with cheer. The

WORDS and MUSIC: Andy Park

7   Let Us Go to the House of the Lord   *Psalm 122:1*

I was glad when they said to me, "Let us
go to the house of the Lord." I was glad when they
said to me, "Let us go to the house of the Lord."

1. Called from ev - 'ry na - tion, called from ev - 'ry race,
2. Here the poor are welcomed, here the lost are claimed.
3. Words that must be spo - ken, grace that must be heard,

gath-ered here for wor - ship in this ho - ly place.
Bro - ken lives are mend-ed; deep - est fears are named.
mer - cy and for - give - ness from God's ho - ly Word

God is here a - mong us; lift your hearts and sing;
Here the wise are child-ren, and the weak are strong.
here will be re - peat - ed, peace to all pro-claimed,

make the walls and raf - ters ring.
Here, in Christ, we all be - long.
shout - ed out in Je - sus' name.

WORDS: Lutheran Book of Worship
MUSIC: Jay Beech

Words © 1978 Lutheran Book of Worship, admin. Augsburg Fortress.
Music © 1995 Augsburg Fortress. Used by permission.

Cántalo

WORDS and MUSIC: Victor Eduardo Jortack, trans. Bret Hesla

9 New Song (Number Forty)

Psalm 40:1–3

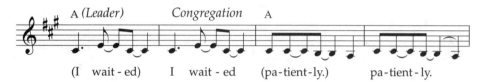

(I wait-ed) I wait-ed (pa-tient-ly.) pa-tient-ly.

(I wait-ed) I wait-ed (for you to hear me.) you to hear me.

(You lis-ten,) You lis-ten, (you heard my cry.) you

heard my cry. (You lift me) You lift me

(high-er and high-er.) high-er and high-er. You give me a new

song; you give me a new song; you give me a new

song to sing!

WORDS and MUSIC: Andra Moran/Josh Elson

Better Is One Day

Psalm 84

WORDS and MUSIC: Matt Redman

11

I'm So Glad

WORDS and MUSIC: Dan Paul

12   The Life You Want to Know

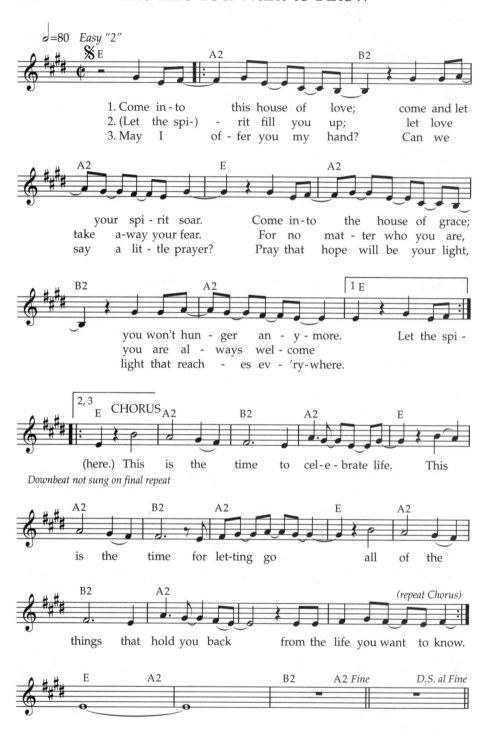

1. Come in-to this house of love; come and let your spi-rit soar. Come in-to the house of grace; you won't hun-ger an-y-more. Let the spi-

2. (Let the spi-) - rit fill you up; let love take a-way your fear. For no mat-ter who you are, you are al-ways wel-come

3. May I of-fer you my hand? Can we say a lit-tle prayer? Pray that hope will be your light, light that reach - es ev-'ry-where.

CHORUS

(here.) This is the time to cel-e-brate life. This

Downbeat not sung on final repeat

is the time for let-ting go all of the

(repeat Chorus)

things that hold you back from the life you want to know.

Fine   *D.S. al Fine*

WORDS and MUSIC: Andra Moran

Come to the Table Again

♩=104

1,4. We're all wel - come. We're all in -
2. We're all cho - sen. We're all God's
3. We're all grate - ful. We're back from

vi - ted. We're all loved ones as we
child - ren. We're all hope - ful as we
where we've been. We're all a - ble to come

Last time to Coda

come to the ta - ble a - gain.
come to the ta - ble a - gain.
back to the ta - ble a - gain.

CHORUS

Come on

in to wor - ship, come on in and share God's

love, come on in, let's get to - ge - ther in the

CODA

place that un - i - fies us.

1st time to Vs. 3
2nd time to Vs. 4

As we

come to the ta - ble a - gain. As we

WORDS and MUSIC: Andra Moran

14 Step by Step

Psalm 63:1–4

♩=104 *Majestically*

O God, you are my God, and I will ev-er praise you.

you. I will seek you in the morn - ing, and I will

learn to walk in your way; and step by step you'll lead

me, and I will fol - low you all of my days.

days. And step by step you'll lead me, and I will

fol - low you all of my days.

WORDS and MUSIC: Beaker

Great Is the Lord

1. Great is the Lord; He is ho-ly and just. By His pow-er we trust in His
2. Great are You, Lord; You are ho-ly and just. By Your pow-er we trust in Your

love. Great is the Lord; He is faith-ful and true. By His
love. Great are You, Lord; You are faith-ful and true. By Your

mer-cy He proves He is love. Great is the Lord and
mer-cy You prove You are love. Great are You, Lord, and

wor-thy of glo-ry! Great is the Lord and wor-thy of praise.
wor-thy of glo-ry! Great are You, Lord, and wor-thy of praise.

Great is the Lord; now lift up your voice; now lift up your voice:
Great are You, Lord; I lift up my voice; I lift up my voice:

Great is the Lord!
Great are You, Lord!

Great is the Lord!
Great are You, Lord!

WORDS and MUSIC: Deborah D. Smith and Michael W. Smith

16 High and Exalted

You are high and ex - alt - ed and wor -

thy of praise; with our hearts we will love and a - dore;

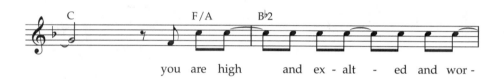

you are high and ex - alt - ed and wor -

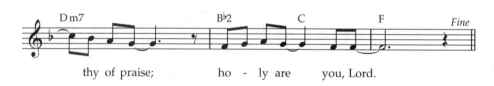

thy of praise; ho - ly are you, Lord.

Ho - ly, ho - ly, ho - ly are you, Lord.

Ho - ly, ho - ly,

ho - ly are you, Lord. You are high

WORDS and MUSIC: Kyle Rasmussen

My Life Is in You, Lord

WORDS and MUSIC: Daniel Gardner

18   Almighty

Psalm 148:7–13

Al-might-y, most ho-ly God, faith-ful through the ag-es; al-might-y, most ho-ly Lord, glo-ri-ous, al-might-y God.

1. The beasts of the field, the birds of the air, are si-lent to call out your name. The earth has no voice, and I have no choice but to mag-ni-fy you un-a-

2. Well, time march-es on, with the in-no-cence gone, and a dark-ness has cov-ered the earth; but your Spir-it dwells and speaks "it is well," with the hope-less still of-fered new

WORDS and MUSIC: Wayne Watson

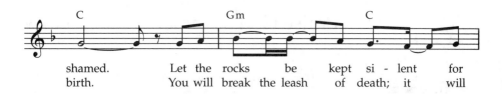

shamed. Let the rocks be kept si - lent for
birth. You will break the leash of death; it will

D.C. al Fine

one more day. Let the whole world sing out; let the peo - ple say:
have no sting. Let the pris - 'ner go free; join the dance and sing:

Philippians 3:7–8

Everything I Am

19

Ev - 'ry-thing I am, ev - 'ry-thing I have,

ev - 'ry-thing I can I bring to you.

For you a - lone are wor-

thy, so I come to give you praise, and

Repeat as desired

ev - 'ry-thing I am I bring to you.

WORDS and MUSIC: Joe Horness and Scott Dyer

20   Praise God's Name

Psalm 100

Make a joy-ful noise to the Lord, all the earth. Come,

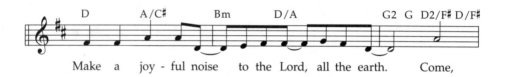

wor-ship with glad - ness. Come in - to God's

pre-sence with sing - ing and *f* praise God's name!

Praise God's ho - ly name! Praise God's name for-ev -

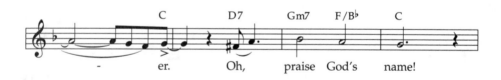

- er. Oh, praise God's name!

Praise God's ho - ly name! Praise God's

WORDS and MUSIC: Stephen Reinhardt

name,   all   the   earth!

En-ter his gates   with thanks - giv - ing   and   his   courts   with

laugh - ter   and   danc - ing.   Come   in - to   God's

pres-ence with sing - ing and   name,   all   the   earth!

Psalm 100

1   Make a joyful noise to the Lord, all the earth.
2   **Serve the Lord with gladness;**
     come into God's presence with singing.
3   Know that the Lord is God.
     It is God who made us, to whom we belong;
     we are God's people, and the sheep of God's pasture.
4   Enter God's gates with thanksgiving,
     and God's courts with praise.
     Give thanks and bless God's name.
5   For the Lord is good;
     God's steadfast love endures forever,
     God's faithfulness to all generations.

21

Hallelujah
(Your Love Is Amazing)

Your love is a-maz - ing, stead-y and un-chang - ing.

Your love is a moun - tain firm be-neath my feet. Your love is a mys-

t'ry, how you gen-tly lift me. When I am sur-round-ed, your love car-ries me.

Hal-le-lu - jah, hal-le-lu - jah, hal-le-lu - jah,

your love makes me sing. And hal-le-lu - jah, hal-le-lu-

jah, hal-le-lu - jah, your love makes me sing.

3rd time to Coda

1. Your love is sur-pris - ing; I can feel it ris-
2. Your love is a-maz - ing, stead-y and un-chang-

ing, all the joy that's grow - ing deep in-side of me.
ing. Your love is a moun - tain firm be-neath my feet.

22   Your Everlasting Love   *Isaiah 54:8–10*

1. Your ev - er-last-ing love   is   high - er,
(2.) - er-last-ing love   is   deep - er,
(3). - er-last-ing love   is   reach - ing,

high - er,   high - er than the sky. Your ev -
deep - er,   deep - er than the sea. Your ev -
reach - ing,   reach - ing out to me. Your ev -

er - last-ing love   is   high - er,
er - last-ing love   is   deep - er,
er - last-ing love   is   reach - ing,

high - er,   high - er than the
deep - er,   deep - er than the
reach - ing,   reach - ing out to

sky,   high - er than the sky.
sea,   deep - er than the sea.
me,   reach - ing out to me.

Oh, the won-der of your ev-er-last-ing love is high-er than the
Oh, the won-der of your ev-er-last-ing love is deep-er than the
Oh, the won-der of your ev-er-last-ing love is reach-ing out to

WORDS and MUSIC: Bill Batstone

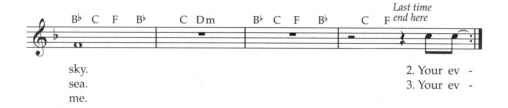

sky.
sea.
me.

2. Your ev -
3. Your ev -

Psalm 96:1–4

I Sing Praises

23

1. I sing prais-es to your name, O Lord, prais-es to your
2. I give glo-ry to your name, O Lord, glo-ry to your

name, O Lord, for your name is great and great-ly to be
name, O Lord, for your name is great and great-ly to be

praised; I sing prais-es to your name, O
praised; I give glo-ry to your name, O

Lord, prais-es to your name,
Lord, glo-ry to your name, O Lord, for your

name is great and great - ly to be praised.

WORDS and MUSIC: Terry Macalmon

24   Sing to the Lord a New Song   *Psalm 47:1–7*

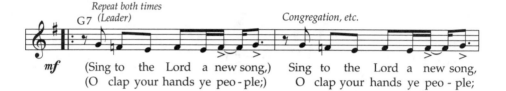

(Sing to the Lord a new song,) Sing to the Lord a new song,
(O clap your hands ye peo-ple;) O clap your hands ye peo-ple;

(a lit-tle rhy-thm for the Lord's de - light!)
(keep sing-in' 'til it feels just right!)

a lit-tle rhy-thm for the Lord's de - light!
keep sing-in' 'til it feels just right!

(Sing to the Lord a new song,) Sing to the Lord a new song,
(O clap your hands ye peo-ple;) O clap your hands ye peo-ple;

(2nd & 4th times grad. cresc.)
(praise him day and night!) praise him day and night!

(Sing a new song!) Sing a new song! (Shout!) Shout! Shout it from the moun-tain!

WORDS and MUSIC: Stephen Reinhardt

(Sing a new song!) Sing a new song! (Shout) Shout in the val-ley be-low!

(Sing a new song!) Sing a new song! (Shout!) Shout! Tell the old sto-ry!

(Sing it!) Sing it! (Shout it!) Shout it! Hon-or and praise to the king of glo-ry!

(Sing it!) Sing it! (Shout it!) Shout it! (Sing it!) Sing it! (Shout it!) Shout it!

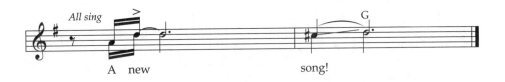

A new song!

Psalm 47:1–2, 5–7

¹ Clap your hands, all you peoples!
  Shout to God with loud songs of joy!
² **For the Lord, the Most High, is awesome,**
  a great Ruler over all the earth.
⁵ God has gone up with a shout,
  the Lord with the sound of a trumpet.
⁶ **Sing praises to God, sing praises!**
  Sing praises to our Ruler, sing praises!
⁷ For God is the Ruler of all the earth.
  Sing praises with a psalm!

25 Blessed Be the Lord God Almighty *Rev. 1:8, 11:17*

WORDS and MUSIC: Bob Fitts

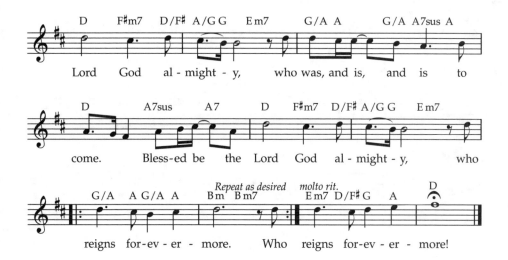

Lord God al-might-y, who was, and is, and is to come. Bless-ed be the Lord God al-might-y, who reigns for-ev-er-more. Who reigns for-ev-er-more!

Repeat as desired *molto rit.*

Psalm 146:1–2

Praise You

26

CAPO: I

♩=84

Praise you, praise you, praise you. Let my life praise you. Praise you, praise you, praise you. Let my life, O Lord, praise you. Praise you. Let my life, O Lord, praise you!

WORDS and MUSIC: Elizabeth Goodine

27 All Things Are Possible

Mark 10:27
Psalm 18:2–3

𝅗𝅥=132 *With energy*

Al-might-y God, my re-deem-er, my hid-ing place,

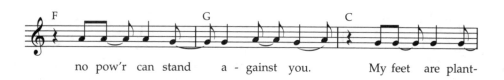

my safe ref-uge. No oth-er name like Je-sus;

no pow'r can stand a-gainst you. My feet are plant-

-ed on this rock, and I will not be shak-en.

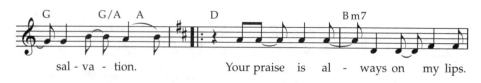

My hope, it comes from you a-lone, my Lord and my

sal-va-tion. Your praise is al-ways on my lips.

WORDS and MUSIC: Darlene Zschech

28   Everything That Has Breath

Psalm 150

1. Praise him in the sanc - tu - a - ry,
2. Praise him in his awe - some po - wer,

praise him in the migh - ty heav - ens. Praise him,
praise his great and ho - ly name. Praise him,

1. all the earth, praise him.

2. the whole world, praise him. From the

ris - ing of the sun let his praise be heard.

From the east to the west and the north to south.

WORDS and MUSIC: Reuben Morgan

29   Lord Most High

Psalm 148

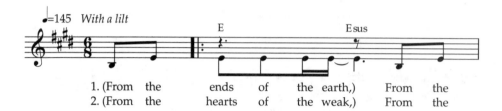

♩=145 *With a lilt*

1. (From the ends of the earth,) From the
2. (From the hearts of the weak,) From the

ends of the earth, (from the depths of the sea,) from the
hearts of the weak, (from the shouts of the strong,) from the

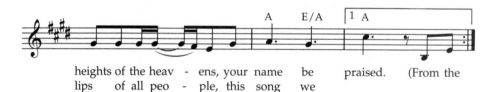

depths of the sea, (from the heights of the heav-ens,) from the
shouts of the strong, (from the lips of all peo-ple,) from the

heights of the heav - ens, your name be praised. (From the
lips of all peo - ple, this song we

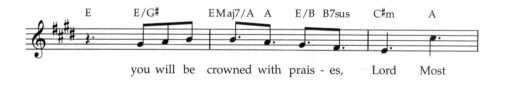

raise, Lord. Through-out the end - less ag - es

you will be crowned with prais - es, Lord Most

WORDS and MUSIC: Don Harris and Gary Sadler

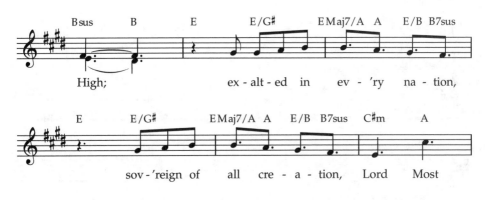

High; ex - alt - ed in ev - 'ry na - tion,

sov - 'reign of all cre - a - tion, Lord Most

High, be mag - ni - fied.

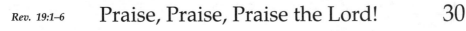

Praise, Praise, Praise the Lord! 30

Rev. 19:1–6

♩=90 *Sing a capella*

C(no 3rd)

Praise, praise, praise the Lord! Praise God's ho - ly name. Al - le-lu - ia!
Lou - ez le Sei-gneur! Lou - ez son saint nom. Al - le-lu - ia!

Praise, praise, praise the Lord! Praise God's ho - ly name. Al - le-lu - ia!
Lou - ez le Sei-gneur! Lou - ez son saint nom. Al - le-lu - ia!

PraiseGod's ho - ly name. Al - le-lu - ia! Praise God's ho - ly name. Al-le-lu - ia!
Lou - ez son saint nom. Al - le-lu - ia! Lou - ez son saint nom. Al - le-lu - ia!

Praise God's ho - ly name. Al-le-lu - ia! Praise God's ho - ly name. Al-le-lu - ia!
Lou - ez son saint nom. Al-le-lu - ia! Lou - ez son saint nom. Al-le-lu - ia!

WORDS and MUSIC: Cameroon processional song,
collected by Elaine Hanson, arr. Ralph M. Johnson

31

All Hail King Jesus

1 Timothy 6:13–16

All hail King Je - sus! All hail Em - man - u - el, King of kings, Lord of lords, Bright Morn - ing Star. And through - out e - ter - ni - ty I'll sing your prais - es, and I'll reign with you through - out e - ter - ni - ty.

WORDS and MUSIC: Dave Moody

32

Celebrate the Lord of Love

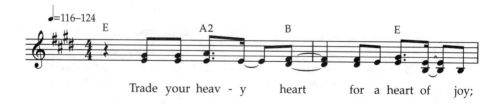

Trade your heav - y heart for a heart of joy;

WORDS and MUSIC: Paul Baloche, Ed Kerr

33   Pure Joy

WORDS and MUSIC: Chris Falson

I Have a Hope

34

I have a hope that will ne - ver fade a - way.

He's a - live in me, li-ving day

to day. I have a hope,

and my hope has a name:

Prince of Peace and the Lord of Love.

Je - sus Christ the Son of God,

King of Hope he will al - ways be. His great

name holds my des - ti - ny!

WORDS and MUSIC: Jim Firth; Arr: Steve Staicoff

35   Shout to the Lord

Psalm 47

My Je - sus,   my Sav - ior,   Lord, there is none   like   you.

All of my days   I want to praise   the won - ders of your

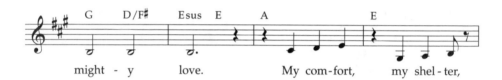

might - y   love.   My com - fort,   my shel - ter,

tow - er of ref - uge and strength,   let ev - ery breath,

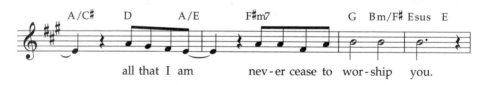

all that I am   nev - er cease to wor - ship   you.

Shout to   the Lord,   all the earth,   let us sing

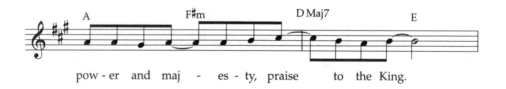

pow - er and maj - es - ty, praise   to the King.

WORDS and MUSIC: Darlene Zschech

Moun-tains bow down, and the seas will roar at the sound of your name. I sing for joy at the work of your hands; for - ev - er I'll love you, for - ev - er I'll stand. Noth-ing com - pares to the prom - ise I have in you.

36   Your People Sing Praises

WORDS and MUSIC: Russell Fragar

37   Open the Eyes of My Heart

Ephesians 1:18

WORDS and MUSIC: Paul Baloche

Another Song about Jesus

For soloist's verses, see full music edition.

WORDS and MUSIC: Michael Carlson

39   Shine, Jesus, Shine   *Revelation 22:1–7*

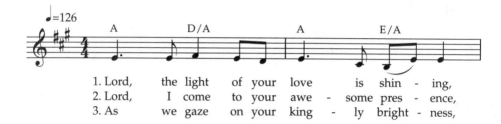

1. Lord, the light of your love is shin - ing,
2. Lord, I come to your awe - some pres - ence,
3. As we gaze on your king - ly bright - ness,

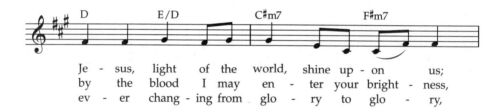

in the midst of the dark - ness shin - ing;
from the sha - dows in - to your ra - di - ance;
so our fac - es dis - play your like - ness;

Je - sus, light of the world, shine up - on us;
by the blood I may en - ter your bright - ness,
ev - er chang - ing from glo - ry to glo - ry,

set us free by the truth you now bring us.
search me, try me, con - sume all my dark - ness.
mir - ror'd here may our lives tell your sto - ry.

Shine on me, shine on me.
Shine on me, shine on me.
Shine on me, shine on me.

WORDS and MUSIC: Graham Kendrick

Shine, Je - sus, shine, fill this land with the

Fa - ther's glo - ry; blaze, Spir - it, blaze, set our hearts on

fire. Flow, riv - er flow, flood the na - tions with

grace and mer-cy. Send forth your word, Lord, and let there be light.

Shout to the North

Luke 13:29

1. Men of faith, rise up and sing of the great and glo-rious King. You are strong when you feel weak, in your bro-ken-ness com-plete.

(2. Rise up,) wo-men of the truth, stand and sing to bro-ken hearts who can know the heal-ing pow'r of our awe-some King of love.

(3. Rise up,) church with bro-ken wings, fill this place with songs a-gain of our God who reigns on high. By His grace a-gain we'll fly.

CHORUS

Shout to the north and the south; sing to the east and the west. Je-sus is Sav-ior to all, Lord of heav-en and earth.

last time to Coda

WORDS and MUSIC: Martin Smith

2. Rise up,
3. Rise up,

We've been through fire;

we've been through rain; we've been re - fined by the

pow'r of His name. We've fall-en deep-er in love with You.

You've burned the truth on our lips.

CODA
Lord of heav-en and earth, Lord

of heav-en and earth.

41   Hear Our Praises

WORDS and MUSIC: Reuben Morgan

fill the air.

3rd time to Bridge

air. From the

BRIDGE
1st time–instruments only

Hal - le - lu - jah! Hal - le - lu - jah!

Hal - le - lu - jah! Hal - le - lu - jah!

D.S. al Coda CODA

From the fill the air.

---

2 Thessalonians 1:12 **Lord, Be Glorified** 42

In my life, Lord, be glo - ri - fied, be glo - ri - fied.

In my life, Lord, be glo - ri - fied to - day.

2. In your church   3. In our praise   4. In our work   5. In our prayers

WORDS and MUSIC: Bob Kilpatrick

43   Praise Him

Psalm 113:3

Praise him! Praise him! Praise him! Praise him!
Glo - ry! Glo - ry! In all things give him glo - ry.

Je - sus, bless-ed Sav - ior, he's wor-thy to be praised.

VERSE 1
From the ris - ing of the sun un - til the
go - ing down of the same, he's wor - thy, Je-sus is
wor - thy, he's wor - thy to be praised.

VERSE 2
God is our rock, hope of sal - va - tion, a
strong de - liv-er-er. In him will I al-ways trust.

WORDS and MUSIC: Donnie Harper

Open Our Eyes, Lord

O - pen our eyes, Lord; we want to see

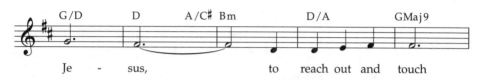

Je - sus, to reach out and touch

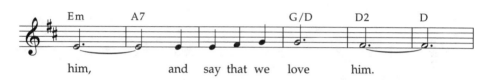

him, and say that we love him.

O - pen our ears, Lord, and help us to

lis - ten. O - pen our eyes,

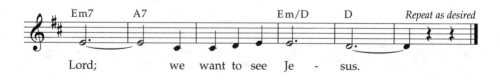

Lord; we want to see Je - sus.

WORDS and MUSIC : Bob Cull

45   No Greater Love

John 15:13

There's no great-er love than Je - sus';

there's no great-er love than he gives.

There's no great-er love that frees us

so deep with-in.   There's no great-er love than

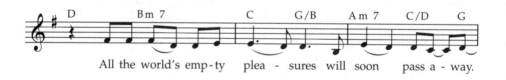

All the world's emp-ty plea - sures will soon pass a - way.

But his love will last for - ev - er; in my

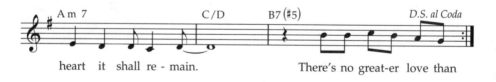

heart it shall re - main.   There's no great-er love than

WORDS and MUSIC: Tommy Walker

46   Think about His Love

Psalm 57:9–10

WORDS and MUSIC: Walt Harrah

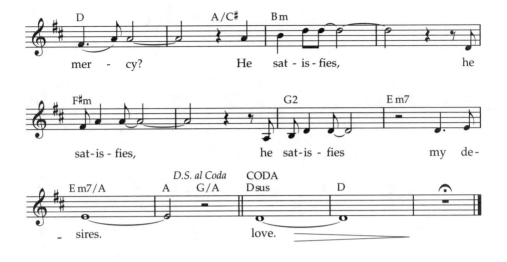

mer - cy? He sat - is - fies, he

sat - is - fies, he sat - is - fies my de-

sires. love.

Psalm 34:15 # O Lord, You're Beautiful — 47

O Lord, you're beau - ti - ful. Your

face is all I seek. For

when your eyes are on this child, your

grace a - bounds to me.

WORDS and MUSIC: Keith Green

48 Sweet Presence of Jesus

WORDS and MUSIC: Tommy Walker

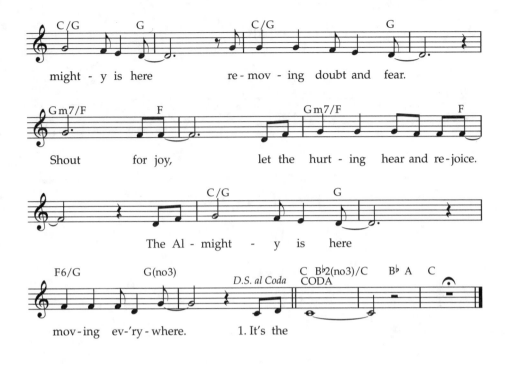

might - y is here re-mov-ing doubt and fear.

Shout for joy, let the hurt-ing hear and re-joice.

The Al - might - y is here

mov-ing ev-'ry-where. 1. It's the

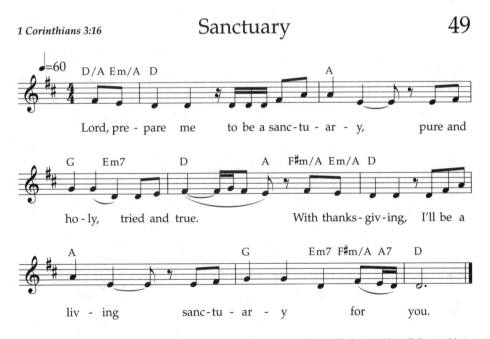

1 Corinthians 3:16

Sanctuary

♩=60

Lord, pre - pare me to be a sanc-tu - ar - y, pure and

ho - ly, tried and true. With thanks - giv-ing, I'll be a

liv - ing sanc-tu - ar - y for you.

WORDS and MUSIC: John Thompson and Randy Scruggs

Majesty

Jude 25

Maj - es - ty, wor-ship his maj - es - ty. Un-to

Je - sus be all glo - ry, hon-or, and praise.

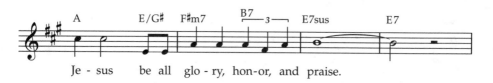

Maj - es - ty, king-dom au - thor - i - ty

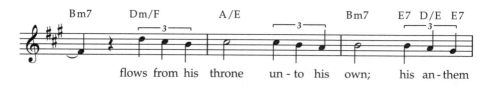

flows from his throne un - to his own; his an-them

raise. So ex - alt, lift up on high the name of

Je - sus. Mag - ni - fy, come glo - ri -

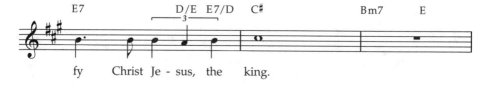

fy Christ Je - sus, the king.

WORDS and MUSIC: Jack Hayford

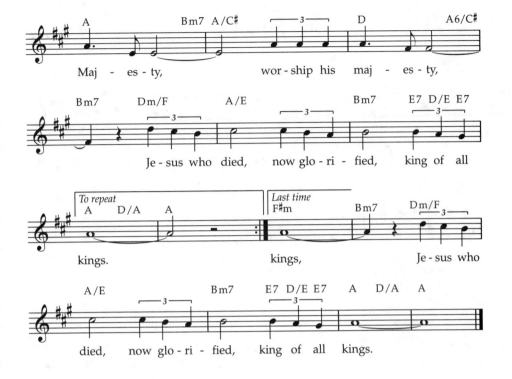

Maj - es - ty, wor - ship his maj - es - ty,

Je - sus who died, now glo - ri - fied, king of all

To repeat *Last time*

kings. kings, Je - sus who

died, now glo - ri - fied, king of all kings.

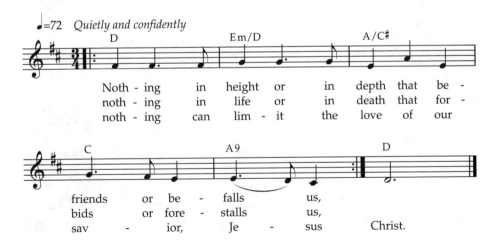

Romans 8:38–39

Nothing in Height

51

♩ =72 *Quietly and confidently*

Noth - ing in height or in depth that be -
noth - ing in life or in death that for -
noth - ing can lim - it the love of our

friends or be - falls us,
bids or fore - stalls us,
sav - ior, Je - sus Christ.

WORDS: Romans 8:38–39 para: John L. Bell
MUSIC: John L. Bell

52

Still Small Voice

1 Kings 19:11–13

WORDS and MUSIC: Thom Schuyler

D.S. CODA   Dsus

3. My   One shout, and the wat-

mp

- ers part - ed,   but he speaks   to the

C

bro - ken - heart - ed with a still   small   voice,

mf G

with a still   small   voice,

C   D7

with a still   small   voice,

G   D   G

than his still   small   voice,

C   D

Em   *rit.*   C   D7

still   small   voice.

p

53 You Are Here

Matthew 18:20

You are here a-mong us, for we have gath-ered in your name. We can feel your pres-ence in this place. You are here a-mong us. You are en-throned up-on our praise. You are here, here to heal and here to save. You are here in our midst; how we've wait-ed for mo-ments like this. Have your way

WORDS and MUSIC: Martin J. Nystrom and Don Moen

in this place, Ho-ly Spir - it, come do as you wish.

We are changed as you move in our midst.

You are here

rit.

Welcome into This Place

54

Wel - come in - to this place. Wel - come in - to this

bro - ken ves - sel. You de - sire to a-bide in the

prais - es of your peo - ple, so we lift our hands and we

lift our hearts as we of-fer up this praise un-to your name.

WORDS and MUSIC: Orlando Juarez

55

This Is Holy Ground

Exodus 3:5

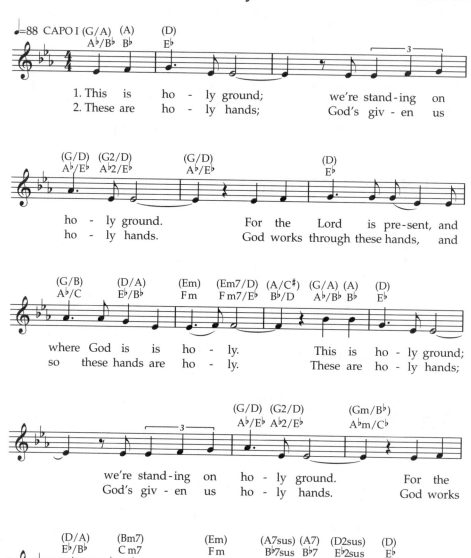

1. This is ho - ly ground; we're stand-ing on
2. These are ho - ly hands; God's giv - en us

ho - ly ground. For the Lord is pre-sent, and
ho - ly hands. God works through these hands, and

where God is is ho - ly. This is ho - ly ground;
so these hands are ho - ly. These are ho - ly hands;

we're stand-ing on ho - ly ground. For the
God's giv - en us ho - ly hands. God works

Lord is pre-sent, and where God is is ho - ly.
through these hands, and so these hands are ho - ly.

WORDS and MUSIC: Christopher Beatty

I Will Celebrate

WORDS and MUSIC: Rita Baloche

57 The Power of Your Love

Isaiah 40:31

1. Lord, I come to you; let my heart be
2. Lord, un-veil my eyes; let me see you

changed, re-newed, flow-ing from the
face - to-face, the know-ledge of your

grace that I've found in
love as you live in

you. And Lord, I've come to know
me. Lord, re-new my mind

the weak-ness-es I see in me
as your will un - folds in my life,

will be stripped a - way
in liv - ing ev - 'ry - day

by the pow'r of your love.
in the pow'r of your love.

WORDS and MUSIC: Geoff Bullock

58   I Could Sing of Your Love Forever   *Psalm 89:1*

O-ver the moun-tains and the sea, your riv-er runs with love for me,

and I will o - pen up my heart and let the Heal - er set me free.

I'm hap-py to be in the truth, and I will dai - ly lift my hands,

for I will al-ways sing of when your love came down, yeah.

I could sing,

I could sing of your love

for - ev - er.

when your love came down, yeah.

WORDS and MUSIC: Martin Smith

59

Jesus, What a Beautiful Name

Philippians 2:5–11

1. Je - sus, what a beau - ti - ful name, Son of God, Son of man, lamb that was slain, joy and peace, strength and hope, grace that blows all fear a - way. Je - sus, what a beau - ti - ful name.

2. Je - sus, what a beau - ti - ful name, truth re - vealed, my fu - ture sealed, healed my pain, love and free - dom, life and warmth,

3. Je - sus, what a beau - ti - ful name, res - cued my soul, my strong - hold, lifts me from shame, for - give - ness, se - cu - ri - ty, pow - er, and love,

name, joy and

* Small notes for verse 3.

WORDS and MUSIC: Tanya Riches

peace, strength and hope, grace that blows all fear a-way.

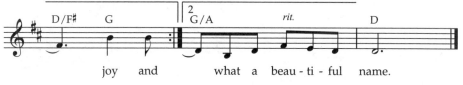

1
G/A

Je - sus, what a beau - ti - ful name,

2
G/A *rit.*

joy and what a beau - ti - ful name.

I Love You, Lord 60

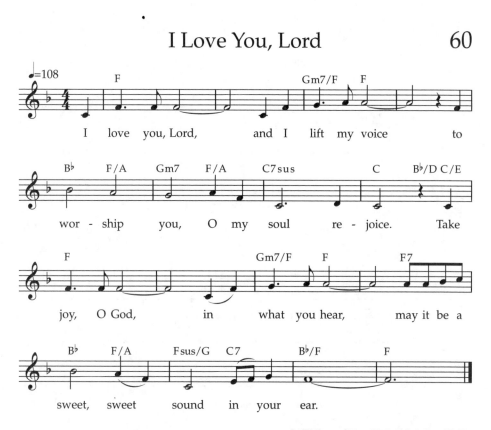

♩=108

I love you, Lord, and I lift my voice to

wor - ship you, O my soul re - joice. Take

joy, O God, in what you hear, may it be a

sweet, sweet sound in your ear.

WORDS and MUSIC: Laurie Klein

61 Shine Down on Me

Psalm 31:16

1. From ev - 'ry moun - tain and o - ver the sea
(2.) I give them all to you.

I shout out your name, Lord, and you're here with me.
It's your peace that guides me, that pulls me through.

When your spir-it falls, it sets me free. When I let,

let your love shine down on me. Shine down on me, shine down on me.

Let the light of your love shine down on me.

2. When bur-dens are heav - y, me.

WORDS and MUSIC: Margaret Davis,
Chris O'Brien, Maria Abraham,
and Carrie Ann Petrillo

Be My Home

Psalm 91:1–2, 14–16

62

WORDS and MUSIC: Handt Hanson and Paul Murakami

© 1996 Changing Church Forum, Inc.

63   O Lord, to You   *Romans 12:1*

WORDS and MUSIC: Gary Sadler

to you. May our wor - ship be a fra -

grance, O Lord, to you.

We will seek you

Proverbs 8:10–11

More Precious than Silver

64

♩=116

Lord, you are more pre-cious than sil-ver.

Lord, you are more cost-ly than gold.

Lord, you are more beau-ti-ful than dia-monds, and

noth-ing I de-sire com-pares with you.

WORDS and MUSIC: Lynn DeShazo

65

Psalm 23

♩=132

C

C

You are my shep-herd. You

F   G   C

give me ev'-ry-thing I'll ev-er need. You

F   G   Em

hold my hand and walk with me be-side the gen-tle

F   F   G   C

stream. You breathe new life in me.

C   C

1. And when I shall walk in the
(2. You) make me a meal in front of

C   F   G

shad-ow,   I will not be a-fraid.
all of my en-emies, and bless-ings o-ver-flow.

WORDS and MUSIC: Andra Moran

Mourning into Dancing

Psalm 30:11–12

WORDS and MUSIC: Tommy Walker

We Fall Down

WORDS and MUSIC: Chris Tomlin

68   Lord of All

1. Lord, I long to see you glor-i-fied in ev-'ry thing I do. All my heart-felt dreams I put a-side to see your spir-it move with pow-er in my life.

2. Je-sus, Lord of all e-ter-ni-ty, your chil-dren rise in faith. All the earth dis-plays your glo-ry, and each word you speak brings life to all who hear. Lord of all, all of cre-a-tion sings your praise in heav-en and earth. Lord, we stand, hearts o-pen wide, be ex-al-ted.

WORDS and MUSIC: Stephen McPherson

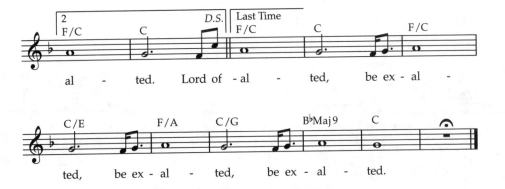

al - ted. Lord of - al - ted, be ex - al -

ted, be ex - al - ted, be ex - al - ted.

Colossians 3:15

Come and Fill

69

♩=76 *With reverence*

Come and fill our hearts with your peace.

You a - lone, O Lord, are ho - ly.

Come and fill our hearts with your peace,

al - le - lu - ia!

WORDS and MUSIC: Taizé

70

In the Secret

♩=100 *With drive*

1. In the se - cret, in the qui - et place,
2. I am reach - ing for the high - est goal

in the still - ness you are there.
that I might re - ceive the prize.

In the se - cret, in the qui - et hour
Press-ing on - ward, push-ing ev - 'ry hin -

I wait on - ly for you, 'cause I want to
drance a - side, out of my way, 'cause I want to

know you more.
know you more.

CHORUS
I want to know you.

I want to hear your voice. I want to know you

more. I want to touch you.

WORDS and MUSIC: Andy Park

I want to see your face. I want to

know you more. more.

Luke 4:16–21
Philippians 2:9–11

Jesus, Your Name

71

1. Je - sus, your name is pow - er;
2. Je - sus, your name is heal - ing;
3. Je - sus, your name is ho - ly;

Je - sus, your name is might.
Je - sus, your name gives sight.
Je - sus, your name brings light.

Je - sus, your name will break ev - 'ry strong - hold;
Je - sus, your name will free ev - 'ry cap - tive;
Je - sus, your name a - bove ev - 'ry oth - er,

Je - sus, your name is life.
Je - sus, your name is life.
Je - sus, your name is life.

WORDS: Morris Chapman
MUSIC: Claire Cloninger

72

Humble Thyself

James 4:10

Hum-ble thy - self in the sight of the Lord.
(Echo) Hum-ble thy-self in the sight of the

Hum-ble thy - self in the sight of the Lord and
Lord.
(Echo) Hum-ble thy-self in the sight of the Lord.

God will lift you up high-er and high - er. And
and God will lift

God will lift you up.
and God will lift

Dm Am7 | *Final time* Dm Am7 Dm Am7 D

up.

WORDS and MUSIC: Bob Hudson

73

More Love, More Power

Mark 12:30

More love, more pow - er,

WORDS and MUSIC: Jude Del Hierro

74 In the Garden

John 20:1–18

♩=64 *Gentle folk guitar style*

1. I come to the gar - den a - lone while the
(2. He) speaks, and the sound of his voice is so

dew is still on the ro - ses, and the
sweet the birds hush their sing - ing, and the

voice I hear fall-ing on my ear, the
mel - o - dy that he gave to me with-

Son of God dis-clo - ses. And he
in my heart is ring - ing.

CHORUS

walks with me, and he talks with me, and he

tells me I am his own, and the

WORDS: C. Austin Miles, 1913
MUSIC: Stephen Reinhardt

Music: © 1995 Stephen Reinhardt

O Redeeming One

Luke 1:68–69, 78–79

1. Je-sus, you are light in the dark - est place; in a world of sor-row you're my song of praise. You're the sac-ri-fice that has saved my soul; you're the heal-ing balm that has made me whole. O re-deem-ing one! You have set me free, for you know me well, yet you still love me. I will sing your praise 'til your face I see! Then I'll be with you, and you'll be with me. me.

2. Je-sus, you are hope in a hope - less land; you're my so - lid rock when there's sink - ing sand. You're my shel - ter from eve - ry troub - led storm; in the cold - est night your love keeps me warm.

3. Je-sus, you are truth in a world turned grey; you're the lamp that guides all a - long the way. Though I fall in sin, still you pick me up; when I thirst for you, you will fill my cup.

WORDS and MUSIC: Dan Adler

Wellspring

WORDS and MUSIC: Nancy Lowry

77 The Heart of Worship

1. When the music fades, all is stripped a-way,
and I simply come,
long-ing just to bring some-thing that's of worth
that will touch your heart.
I'll bring you more than a song, for a song in it-self
is not what you have re-quired.
You search much deep-er with-in through the way things ap-pear;

2. King of end-less worth, no one could ex-press
how much you de-serve.
Though I'm weak and poor, all I have is yours,
ev-'ry sin-gle breath.

WORDS and MUSIC: Matt Redman

78

You Are My All in All

2 Corinthians 12:9–10
Colossians 3:11

You are my strength when I am weak; you are the trea-sure that I
Seek-ing you as a pre-cious jewel, Lord, to give up I'd be a

seek; you are my all in all.
fool. You are my all in all!

PART I *(May be sung as a 2-part round)*

(opt. D.S.)

Je - sus, Lamb of God, wor - thy is your

name. Je - sus, Lamb of God,

wor - thy is your name.

PART II

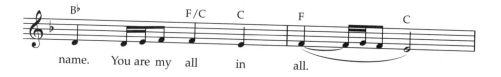

Tak-ing my sin, my cross, my shame, ris-ing a-gain; I bless your

name. You are my all in all.

WORDS and MUSIC: Dennis L. Jernigan

79 And That My Soul Knows Very Well

You make your face to shine on me, and that my soul knows ve-ry well.

You lift me up; I'm cleansed and free, and that my soul knows ve - ry well. When moun-tains fall,

I'll stand by the pow - er of your hand, and in your heart of hearts I'll dwell, and that my soul knows ve - ry well. When moun-tains fall,

Joy and strength each day I'll find, and that my

WORDS and MUSIC: Darlene Zschech and Russell Fragar

80

Unashamed Love

WORDS and MUSIC: Lamont Hiebert

81
Your Love, O God

Psalm 136:1

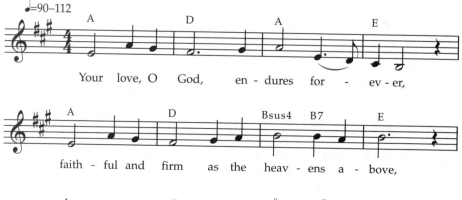

♩=90–112

| A | D | A | E |

Your love, O God, en - dures for - ev - er,

| A | D | Bsus4 B7 | E |

faith - ful and firm as the heav - ens a - bove,

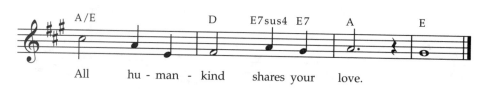

| A | D | C#sus C#7 | F# |

op - 'ning our minds through - out all time.

| A/E | D | E7sus4 E7 | A | E |

All hu - man - kind shares your love.

WORDS and MUSIC: Michael Carlson

82
Make Us One

Galatians 3:28

♩=65

| C | | E/G | G7 CMaj7 | Dm9 |

𝄋 *(opt. D.S.)*

Make us one, Lord, make us

| Em7 | C/E | Gm11 | C G/C C | F2 | F6 | C/D |

one; Ho-ly Spir - it, make us one. Let your

WORDS and MUSIC: Carol Cymbala

love flow   so the world   will   know   we   are   one   in

Repeat ending
C   F/G   G7

D.S.

Song ending
C

you.   Make   us   you.

I Worship You, Almighty God   83

I   wor - ship you,   Al - might - y God;   there is none like

you.   I   wor - ship you,   O   Prince   of Peace;

that is what   I   want   to do.   I   give   you praise,

for you are my   right - eous - ness;   I

wor - ship you,   Al - might - y God;   there is none like   you.

WORDS and MUSIC: Sondra Corbett-Wood

Our Father

Matthew 6:9–13

(Our Fath - er,) Our Fath - er, (who art in

heav - en,) who art in heav - en, (hal-low-ed be thy name.)

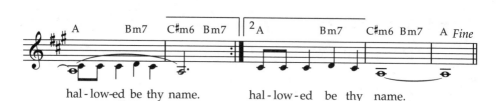

hal - low-ed be thy name.   hal - low-ed be thy name.

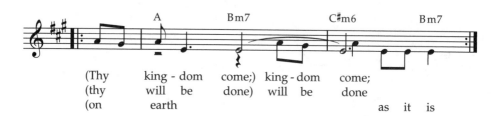

(Thy   king - dom   come;)   king - dom   come;
(thy   will   be   done)   will   be   done
(on   earth   as   it   is

in heav-en.) as it is in heav-en.   (Give   us   this day) Give
(the   food   we need) the
(and for-give   our sins) and for-
(as   we for-give those) as we

MUSIC: unidentified; arr. Jim Strathdee

us this day
food we need
give our sins
for - give those (who sin a-gainst us all.) who sin a-gainst us all.

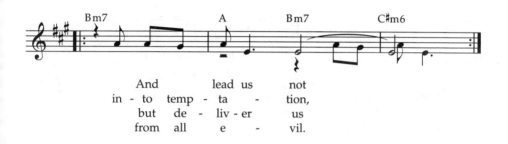

And lead us not
in - to temp - ta - tion,
but de - liv - er us
from all e - vil.

For thine is the king - dom and the

pow-er and the glo-ry for - ev - er.

D.C. al Fine

(For - ev - er) For - ev - er (and ev - er.) and ev - er.

85   Our Father

Matthew 6:9–13

1. Hear our prayer;

(2. Hear our song)   as it ris -

we are your child - ren, and we've gath - ered here to - day.

- es to heav - en; may your glo - ry fill the earth

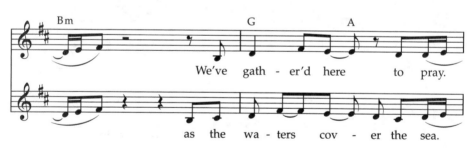

We've gath - er'd here to pray.

as the wa - ters cov - er the sea.

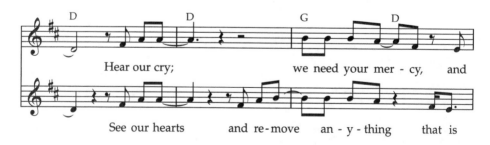

Hear our cry; we need your mer - cy, and

See our hearts and re - move an - y - thing that is

WORDS and MUSIC: Don Moen

© 2000 Integrity's Hosanna! Music/ASCAP. All rights reserved.
International copyright secured. Used by permission.

we'll be sing - ing for-ev-er: Ho - ly is the Lord.

Ho - ly is the Lord. Ho - ly is the Lord.

Ho - ly is the Lord. Ho - ly is the Lord.

Last time to Coda

Ho - ly is the Lord.

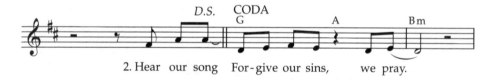

D.S. CODA

2. Hear our song For-give our sins, we pray.

For - give our sins, we pray.

For-give our sins, we pray.

Change My Heart, O God

Change my heart, O God.   Make it ev-er true.

Change my heart, O God.   May I be like you.

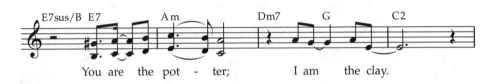

You are the pot - ter;   I am the clay.

Mold me and make me;   this is what I pray.

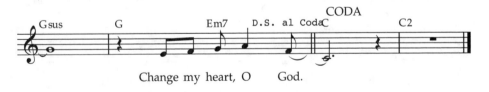

Change my heart, O God.

WORDS and MUSIC: Eddie Espinosa

87

Le lo le lo lay lo
(Sanctus)

Matthew 21:9

Pronounciation in English: le = leh, lay = lie, lo = loh.

WORDS: Sanctus (Holy, Holy, Holy)
MUSIC: William Loperena, O.P., Puerto Rico

Spanish/English editions © 2000 General Board of Global Ministries,
GBGMusik, and Order de Predicadores

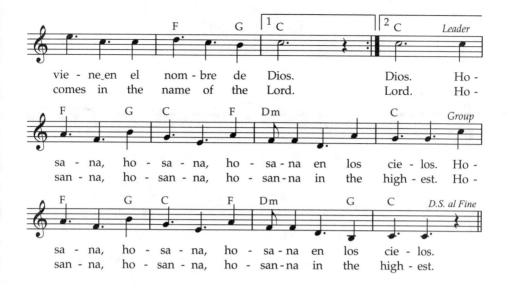

vie - ne en el nom - bre de Dios. Dios. Ho -
comes in the name of the Lord. Lord. Ho -

sa - na, ho - sa - na, ho - sa - na en los cie - los. Ho -
san - na, ho - san - na, ho - san - na in the high - est. Ho -

sa - na, ho - sa - na, ho - sa - na en los cie - los.
san - na, ho - san - na, ho - san - na in the high - est.

Hide Me in Your Holiness

88

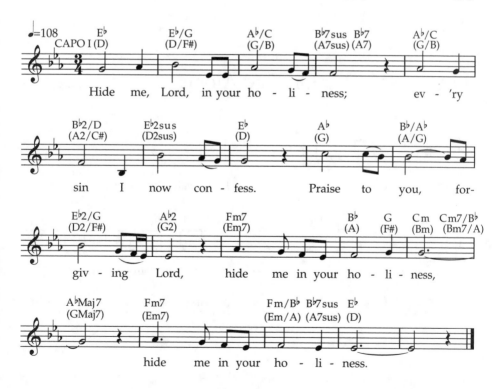

Hide me, Lord, in your ho - li - ness; ev - 'ry

sin I now con - fess. Praise to you, for-

giv - ing Lord, hide me in your ho - li - ness,

hide me in your ho - li - ness.

WORDS and MUSIC: Steve Ragsdale

89

Be Still and Know

Psalm 46:10-11

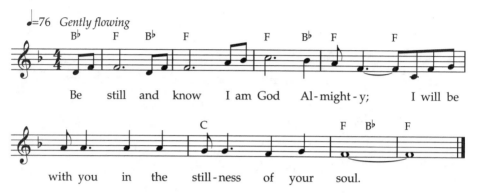

Be still and know I am God Al-might-y; I will be

with you in the still-ness of your soul.

WORDS and MUSIC: Jim Manley

90

On God Alone

Psalm 62:1-2

On God a - lone I wait si - lent - ly,

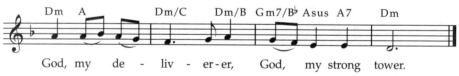

God, my de - liv - er-er, God, my strong tower.

WORDS: Psalm 62:1–2 para: John Bell
MUSIC: John Bell

Create in Me a Clean Heart

WORDS: Psalm 51:10–12
MUSIC: Stephen Reinhardt

Arrangement: © 2003 Stephen Reinhardt

92   Make Me an Instrument of Your Peace

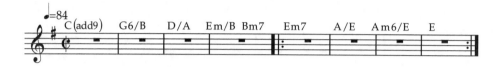

1. Where there is ha - tred, let me bring love;
2. Where there is des - pair - ing, let me bring hope;
4. For it is in giv - ing that we re - ceive,

where there is in - ju - ry, let me bring par - don;
where there is dark - ness, let me bring light;
and it is in par-don-ing that we are par - doned,

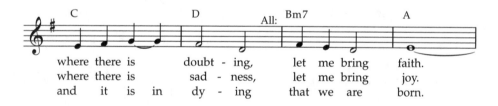

where there is doubt - ing, let me bring faith.
where there is sad - ness, let me bring joy.
and it is in dy - ing that we are born.

CHORUS

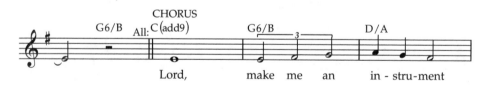

Lord, make me an in - stru - ment

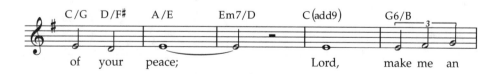

of your peace; Lord, make me an

WORDS: Francis of Assisi, adapt. Marty Haugen
MUSIC: Marty Haugen

93   Your Great Love

Psalm 89:1

1. I will sing of your great love; I will sing of your com-pas-sion; I will sing of all your faith-ful-ness and mer-cy un-to me. I will sing of all you are; I will bow to you in wor-ship; I will find my joy in you a - lone; I will sing of your great love.

2. I will give you all my fears; I will drink of your sal-va-tion; I will dance just like a lit-tle child be-fore my Fath-er's throne. I will seek to hon-or you; I will live in cel-e-bra-tion; I will tell of all you've done for me; I will sing of your great love. Of your

WORDS and MUSIC: John Chisum and Jeff Slaughter

love, of your great love for me, of your

blood's for-giv-ing, heal-ing stream, so

high, so wide, so full, so deep, I will sing of

your great love for me.

John 20:22

Breathe on Me

94

Breathe on me, O breath of God. Grant your life to
Shine on me, O light of God. Grant that I may

me. Make of me a rush - ing wind, come and
see. Make of me a liv - ing light, come and

breathe on me. Come and breathe on me.
shine on me. Come and shine on me.

WORDS and MUSIC: Stephen M. Austin

95   Be Still

Psalm 46:10

1. Too man - y words
2. Too man - y thoughts

don't mean e-nough.
crowd - ing my mind.

How can I say   I
So man - y an - swers   I'm

need you so much?   So I will be
hop - ing to find.

si - lent.   And I will be ver - y still.

And I will be qui - et.   I will

WORDS and MUSIC: Andra Moran and Josh Elson

96   Kyrie

1. (Ky - ri - e e - le - i - son,) Ky - ri - e e - le - i - son,
2. (Chris - te e - le - i - son,) Chris - te e - le - i - son,
3. (Ky - ri - e e - le - i - son,) Ky - ri - e e - le - i - son,

(Lord, have mer - cy,) Lord, have mer - cy, (Christ, have mer - cy,)

Christ, have mer - cy, (Lord, have mer - cy) Lord, have mer - cy

on me.

(Ky - ri - e,)

Ky - ri - e, (Chris - te,) Chris - te, (Ky - ri - e,)

Ky - ri - e, on me.

WORDS and MUSIC: Steven B. Eulberg

You Are Merciful to Me

You are mer-ci-ful to me; you are mer-ci-ful to me; you are

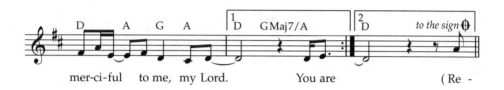

mer-ci-ful to me, my Lord. You are (Re -

- deem - er,) Re-deem - er, (Sav - iour,) Sav - iour,

(Heal-er;) Heal - er;(and Friend.) and Friend. (Ev-'ry day) Ev-'ry day (re-

new my ways,) re-new my ways, (fill me with love) fill me with love (that

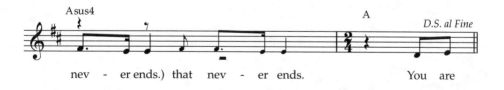

nev - er ends.) that nev - er ends. You are

WORDS and MUSIC: Ian White

98
Good to Me

Psalm 86:4–7, 15

I cry out for your hand of mer-cy to heal me.

I am weak; I need your love to free me, O Lord, my

rock, my strength in weak-ness. Come res - cue me, O

Lord.   Lord.   You are my hope; your

prom-ise nev - er fails me, and my de - sire is to

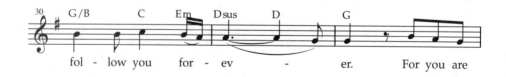

fol - low you for - ev - er. For you are

WORDS and MUSIC: Craig Musseau

good, for you are good, for you are good to me. For you are good, for you are good, for you are good to me. me.

John 13:14–16

Make Me a Servant

99

Make me a ser-vant, hum-ble and meek. Lord, let me lift up those who are weak, and may the prayer of my heart al-ways be: make me a ser-vant, make me a ser-vant, make me a ser-vant to-day.

rit.

WORDS and MUSIC: Kelly Willard

All Good Gifts

Mark 4:26–29

heav-en a-bove.   So thank the

Lord,   O thank   the Lord   for all his love.

We   For all his love.

Joel 2:13

Return to the Lord

101

Re - turn   to the Lord,   your   God;   re -

turn   to   the Lord,   your God,   who   is

gra - cious   and mer - ci - ful,   slow   to an - ger, and a -

bound - ing   in stead - fast   love.

WORDS and MUSIC: Jay Beech   © 1997 Jay Beech. Used by permission of Augsburg Fortress.

102   Let the Peace of God Reign

WORDS and MUSIC: Darlene Zschech

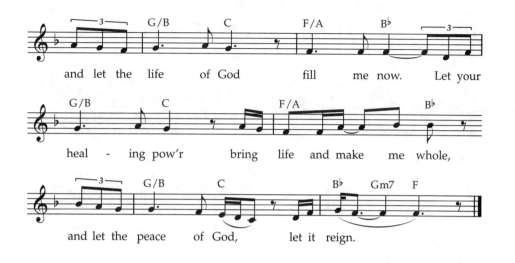

and let the life of God fill me now. Let your

heal - ing pow'r bring life and make me whole,

and let the peace of God, let it reign.

Jeremiah 17:14

Heal Me, O Lord

103

Heal me, O Lord, and I shall be healed; save me, and

I shall be saved. saved.

For you are my praise,

save me, and I shall be saved.

WORDS and MUSIC: Steven B. Eulberg

104   O Lord, Hear My Prayer

Psalm 102:1, 2

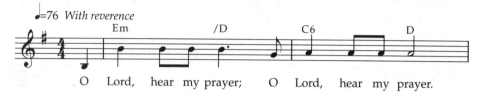

O Lord, hear my prayer; O Lord, hear my prayer.

When I call, an - swer me. O Lord, hear my prayer; O

Lord, hear my prayer. Come and lis - ten to me. The

Lord is my song; the Lord is my praise: All my hope

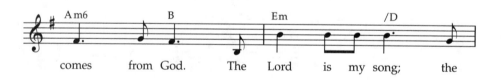

comes from God. The Lord is my song; the

Lord is my praise: God, the well-spring of life.

WORDS and MUSIC: Taizé

River of Mercy

1. Mer - cy, com-pas - sion, kind-ness and love,
2. Thirst-y, hun - gry, strang-ers in need.
3. Je - sus, Son of God, Sav - ior and Lord,

jus - tice, for-give - ness, poured out from a-bove.
Lone - ly, out - cast, pris - on - ers to free.
Might - y Prince of Peace, the One we a-dore.

There's a ri - ver of mer - cy flow-ing on high.

Wa - ters of jus - tice cross the sky. There's a

riv - er of mer - cy that shines in the night, a

riv - er of mer - cy that flows through you and

I.

through our lives.

WORDS and MUSIC: Paul Frantsen

106   You'll Find Love

♩=84

1. For the fail - ures   there's for - give - ness.
2. For the out - cast   there's ac - cept - ance.
3. For the lone - ly   there is friend-ship.

For the bro - ken - ness,   heal - ing for your souls.
For the pris - on - ers,   free-dom from the past.
For the lost,   a   pur-pose in this life.

For the sick - ness   there's   a   cure.
For the thirst - y,   wa - ter for your soul.
For the strang - er, a   place   to call your home.

All who come here will find   love.   You'll find
All who come here will find   love.
All who come here will find   love.

love that's wait - ing   here   for you. It's the

heart of Christ that's ach - ing   here   for you. There's a

fam - i - ly reach-ing out   for you. You'll find   love out-poured.

WORDS and MUSIC: Paul Frantsen

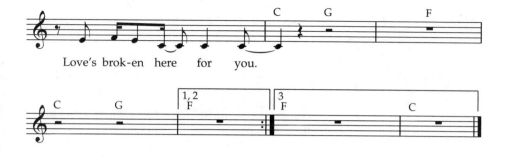

Love's brok-en here for you.

2 Corinthians 5:1 # Lord, Keep Me Day by Day **107**

♩.=58

1. Lord, keep me day by day
2. Lord, keep my bod - y strong
3. I'm just a stran - ger here,

in a pure and per - fect way.
so that I can do no wrong.
trav - 'ling through this bar - ren land.

I want to live, I want to live on
Lord, give me grace just to run this Chris-tian race
Lord, I know there's a build-ing some-where,

in a build - ing not made by hand.
to a build - ing not made by hand.
a build - ing not made by hand.

WORDS and MUSIC: Eddie Williams; arr. Valeria A. Foster

108 As the Deer

Psalm 42:1

1. As the deer pants for the wa-ter, so my soul longs af-ter you. You a-lone are my heart's de-sire, and I long to wor-ship you.
2. You're my friend and you are my broth-er ev-en though you are a king. I love you more than an-y oth-er, so much more than an-y-thing.
3. I want you more than gold or sil-ver; on-ly you can sat-is-fy. You a-lone are the real joy-giv-er and the ap-ple of my eye.

You a-lone are my strength, my shield; to you a-lone may my spir-it yield. You a-lone are my heart's de-sire, and I long to wor-ship you.

WORDS and MUSIC: Martin J. Nystrom

You're Here

1. I tried so hard. I just don't un-der-stand it.
2. I al-ways thought that there must be a rea-son,

I ne-ver thought this could be.
must be a rea-son for pain. But

Day af-ter day it gets hard - er to man-age.
in ev-'ry-thing there comes a sea-son, and

How could this hap - pen to me? But you're
this is the sea - son for rain.

here. You're here. You're all

that I need, the one thing I see that's clear.

Yes, you're here.

WORDS and MUSIC: Andra Moran

110   A Place of Prayer

Matthew 6:5–8

WORDS: Roger Hellwege
MUSIC: Glenn Sulley

Lift Me Up

1. Lift me up, lift me up when I'm down, O my Lord. Lift me up, lift me up when I'm down. Shine your light, see me through, by your strength I am renewed. Lift me up, lift me up when I'm down.

(2. Hold my) hand, hold my hand, when I'm scared, O my Lord. Hold my hand, hold my hand when I'm scared. Shine your light, see me through, by your strength I am renewed. Hold my hand, hold my hand when I'm scared.

(3. Touch my) heart, touch my heart, when I doubt, O my Lord. Touch my heart, touch my heart when I doubt. Shine your light, see me through, by your strength I am renewed. Touch my heart, touch my heart when I doubt.

WORDS and MUSIC: Paul B. Svenson

112   Come Fill Me

Acts 4:31

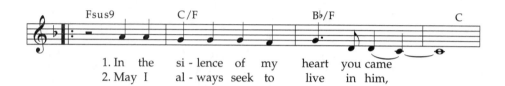

1. In the si - lence of my heart you came
2. May I al - ways seek to live in him,

and o - pened my eyes to your love.
root-ed and built up in his love,

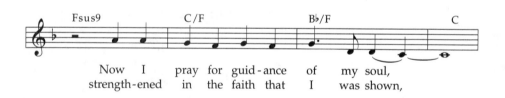

Now I pray for guid - ance of my soul,
strength-ened in the faith that I was shown,

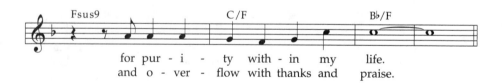

for pur - i - ty with - in my life.
and o - ver - flow with thanks and praise.

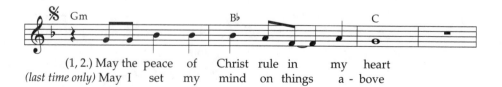

(1, 2.) May the peace of Christ rule in my heart
(last time only) May I set my mind on things a - bove

WORDS and MUSIC: William Campbell

© 1999 William Campbell

113   Jesus, Lover of My Soul

WORDS and MUSIC: John Ezzy,
Daniel Grul, and Stephen McPherson

Take My Life

1. Ho - li - ness, ho - li - ness is what I long for.
2. Faith - ful - ness, faith - ful - ness is what I long for.
3. Right-eous-ness, right-eous-ness is what I long for.

Ho - li - ness is what I need.
Faith - ful - ness is what I need.
Right - eous - ness is what I need.

Ho - li - ness, ho - li - ness is what you want from me.
Faith - ful - ness, faith - ful - ness is what you want from me.
Right-eous-ness, right-eous-ness is what you want from me.

So take my heart and form it; take my

mind, trans-form it; take my will, con-form

it to yours, to yours, O Lord.

WORDS and MUSIC: Scott Underwood

115   Hold Me, Lord

Ecclesiastes 3:1–8

1. The road I've trav - elled   has been ea - sy.
2. But now the storm clouds   gath - er quick - ly.

You've let   the sun shine   on   my   face.
My time   of trial   is   at   hand.

And when I've falt-ered,   you've   held me up.   You have
My days grow end-less,   and the nights so long,   Lord, with-

filled   my   cup   in this time and place.   stand.
out   your song   I   can-not

Hold   me,   hold me,   Lord.   Hold me in   your pre-cious

arms   and   sing   to me   that sweet song   you

WORDS and MUSIC: Stephen Reinhardt

taught me long a-go; you've got-ta hold me now, hold me,

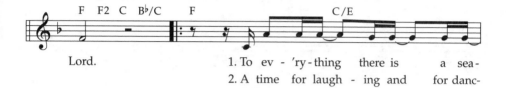

Lord.

1. To ev - 'ry-thing there is a sea-
2. A time for laugh - ing and for danc-

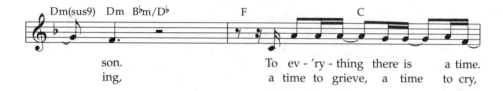

son.

To ev - 'ry - thing there is a time.
ing, a time to grieve, a time to cry,

For ev - 'ry pur - pose un - der heav -
a time to call to mind that

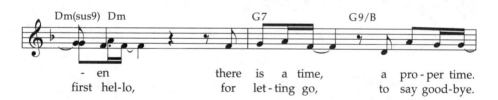

- en there is a time, a pro - per time.
first hel-lo, for let - ting go, to say good-bye.

Lord; you've got-ta hold

me now, hold me, Lord.

116　I Will Sing

Jeremiah 20:13

Lord, you seem so far a-way, a mil-lion miles or more it feels to-day. Though I have-n't lost my faith, I must con-fess right now that it's hard for me to pray. But I don't know what to say, and I don't know where to start. But as you give the grace, with

WORDS and MUSIC: Don Moen

117

Nada Te Turbe
Nothing Can Trouble

Psalm 34:4–6

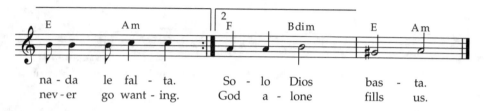

Na - da te tur - be; na - da te_es-pan - te. Quien a Dios tie - ne
Noth-ing can trou-ble; noth-ing can fright-en. Those who seek God shall

na - da le fal - ta. So - lo Dios bas - ta.
nev - er go want - ing. God a - lone fills us.

WORDS: St. Teresa de Jesus/Taizé
MUSIC: Jacques Berthier

118

Waterlife

John 4:10–15

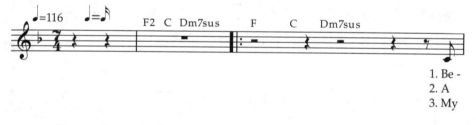

1. Be -
2. A
3. My

fore I can re-mem-ber, the cov - e - nant was sealed with
sim - ple sweet be - gin-ning, a lov - ing place to start,
hope and ex - pec - ta - tion for true com-mun - i - ty be -

WORDS and MUSIC: Handt Hanson

119   What the Lord Has Done in Me   *Matthew 11:4–6*

WORDS and MUSIC: Reuben Morgan

hea - ven's mer - cy stream   of the   Sa - vior's love for me.
sing   sal - va - tion songs.   Je - sus   Christ has   set   me free.

3. I will   Ho - san-na, Ho - san - na to the Lamb that was

slain.   Ho - san-na, Ho - san - na. Je-sus died and rose a - gain.   Ho -

gain.   Je-sus died   and rose a - gain.   Je-sus died   and rose a - gain.

120 Child of the Water

1 John 3:1–3

You're a child of the wa - ter, child of the word,

guid-ed by prom - ise and sto - ries you've heard.

God of the wound - ed knows you by name and

car - ries you home ev' - ry day.

1. From your first breath
2. Life is a gift,

to the last step, all of your life; down
time car - ries on, and you will grow; a -
3. We

deep in your laugh - ter, what - ev - er your fears,
midst your be - liev - ing and through-out your doubt,
jour - ney to - geth - er as child - ren of God,

try to re - mem - ber . . .
some - thing is sure . . .
sealed by the cross . . .

WORDS and MUSIC: Hans Peterson, Larry Olson, and David Lee Brown

Lead Me to the Rock

mf Lead me to the Rock that is high-er than I. Let your ten-der mer-cies be known. Fill me with the song of sal - va-tion, and I will go danc - ing with these bro - ken bones.

1. Purge me, and I will be clean; wash me, and I will be whit - er than snow. Fa - ther, wher - ev - er I go
2. Let ev - 'ry word from my mouth and ev - 'ry thought that col - lects in my heart be wor - thy of how great thou art.

3rd time to Coda

Repeat twice

CODA bones. I will go danc - ing with these bro - ken bones.

WORDS and MUSIC: Thom Schuyler

122   Every Time I Think of You   *Philippians 1:1*

♩=120

1. The Lord has blessed you,   it's plain to see,
2. When I re - mem - ber   all we've been through
3. We've been like part - ners   in all we do;

and I'm so thank-ful for the bless-ing you have been to me,
and how you've helped me, well, my heart is filled with grat - i-tude,
we're on a mis - sion, and I know that I can count on you,

bless-ing you have been to me.
heart is filled with grat - i-tude.
know that I can count on you.

1, 2
C7   B7+5   E

I thank my God ev - 'ry time I think of you.

3
C7   B7+5

I thank my God ev -

- 'ry time I think of you.

WORDS and MUSIC: Jay Beech

4. We've always started down on our knees;
   we say a prayer and then get busy rolling up our sleeves,
      busy rolling up our sleeves.
   I thank my God every time I think of you.

5. We know the Spirit will see it through;
   we plant the seeds and then we wait and see what God will do,
      wait and see what God will do.
   I thank my God every time I think of you.

6. And so I'm praying that you will grow,
   that God will fill you and the love of Jesus overflow,
      love of Jesus overflow.
   I thank my God every time I think of you.

7. I'm sure of one thing: What God began
   will be completed when we enter in the promised land,
      enter in the promised land.
   I thank my God every time I think of you.

Deuteronomy 6:5   ## Love the Lord Your God   **123**

WORDS and MUSIC: Jean and Jim Strathdee

124

Yea, O God

Isaiah 64:8

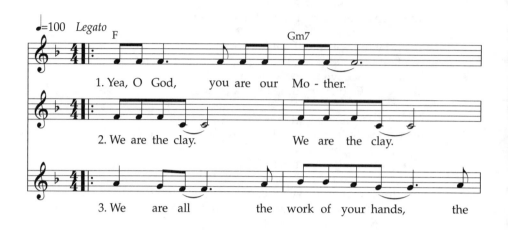

1. Yea, O God, you are our Mo - ther.
2. We are the clay. We are the clay.
3. We are all the work of your hands, the

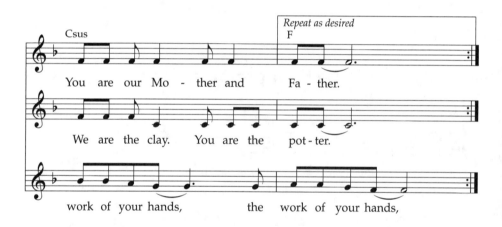

You are our Mo - ther and Fa - ther.
We are the clay. You are the pot - ter.
work of your hands, the work of your hands,

Repeat as desired

Last time

work of your hands.

WORDS and MUSIC: Larry Dittberner

Lord of Justice

Lord of jus - tice, Lord of life, help us to do what you
know is right. Lord of jus - tice, Lord of life,
guide us through the day and night.

1. To the strang - er may we give wel - come; to the
2. To the wound - ed may we give heal - ing; to the

1. hun - gry may we give bread. To the
2. voice - less may we give words. To the

1. nak - ed may we give cloth - ing, to the
2. cap - tives may we give free - dom, to the

1. home - less a place to lay their head.
2. tor - tured re - lease from all the hurt.

WORDS and MUSIC: Larry Olson

126   Through These Hands

Through these hands flows a riv-er of God's grace and mer-cy, jus-tice and fierce-ness of love. Through these hands flows the heal-ing God a-lone can of-fer, flow-ing through these hands.

1. Through these hands flows a ri-ver of God's grace and love. Through these hands flows the heal-ing Je-sus gives to us. Through these hands,

2. It's the way of our free-dom. It's the way of our loss. It's the way of our vic-tory. It's the way of the cross. Through these

3. It's the way of the thirst-y. It's the way that sat-is-fies. It's the way of an out-cast. It's the way of a child. Through these

4. It's the way of com-pas-sion. It's the way of our peace. It's the way of for-give-ness. It's the way of re-lease. Through these hands, flow-ing through these hands.

WORDS and MUSIC: Trish Bruxvoort Colligan and Paul Frantsen

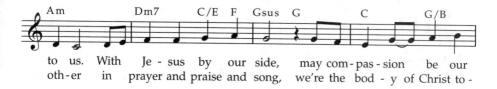

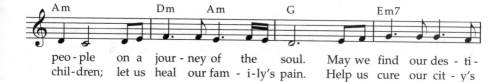

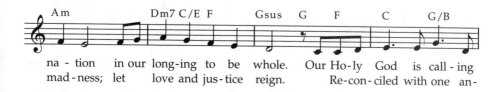

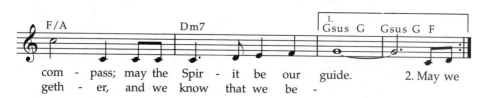

1. We are a wil-der-ness wand-'ring peo-ple on a jour-ney of the soul. May we find our des-ti-na-tion in our long-ing to be whole. Our Ho-ly God is call-ing to us. With Je-sus by our side, may com-pas-sion be our com-pass; may the Spir-it be our guide.

(2. May we) cher-ish all our chil-dren; let us heal our fam-i-ly's pain. Help us cure our cit-y's mad-ness; let love and jus-tice reign. Re-con-ciled with one an-oth-er in prayer and praise and song, we're the bod-y of Christ to-geth-er, and we know that we be-long, we be-long, we be-long, we be-long.

WORDS and MUSIC: Jim Strathdee

128 Cry of My Heart

John 12:26

It is the cry of my heart to fol-low you. It is the cry of my heart
to be close to you. It is the cry of my heart to fol-low
all of the days of my life.

1. Teach me your ho - ly ways, O Lord,
2. O - pen my eyes so I can see the

so I can walk in your truth.
won-der-ful things that you do.

Teach me your ho - ly ways,
O-pen my heart up more

(take 3rd ending)

O Lord, and make me whol-ly de-vot-ed to you. O, O, woh.
and more and make it

WORDS and MUSIC: Terry Butler

129   I Believe in Jesus   *Romans 10:9*

WORDS and MUSIC: Marc Nelson

Je - sus, you're all

I   need;   you're all   I   need.

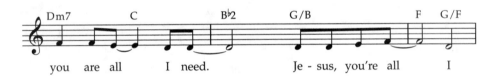

Now I give   my life   to you   a - lone;

you   are all   I   need.   Je - sus, you're all   I

need;   you're all   I   need.   Lord, you gave

your - self   so I   could   live.   You are all   I   need.

WORDS and MUSIC: Darlene Zschech

131 Where Do I Go?

Give Thanks to the Lord

Give thanks to the Lord, for he is good, and his

mer - cy will en - dure. For he a - lone has done mar-

v'lous things, give thanks un-to the Lord. For he

made the earth and hea - ven with a strong and migh-ty hand,

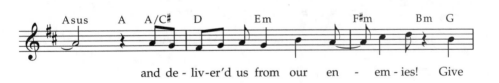

and de - liv-er'd us from our en - em - ies! Give

thanks un - to the Lord. Give

WORDS and MUSIC: Stephen M. Austin

133   I See a Church

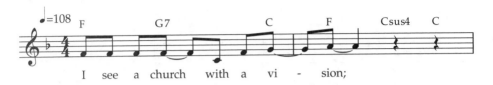

I see a church with a vi - sion;

I see a church on a mis - sion.

CHORUS

I see a church who has made her mind up, and she's build-

- ing her hopes on things e - ter - nal. She's

hold - ing to God's un - chang - ing hand.

I see a church with a vi - sion;

I see a church on a mis - sion.

WORDS and MUSIC: William Thomas, Jr.

have to hide,   and there all   of God's chil - dren can sweet-

ly a - bide,   and there all   of God's chil - dren can sweet-

CODA

ly a - bide.   hand,

hold - ing   to God's   un - chang - ing   hand!

134   Tree of Life

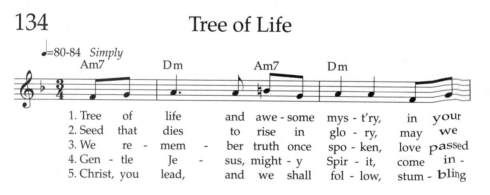

1. Tree   of   life   and awe - some mys - t'ry,   in your
2. Seed   that   dies   to   rise   in   glo - ry,   may we
3. We   re - mem - ber truth once   spo - ken,   love passed
4. Gen - tle   Je - sus, might - y   Spir - it,   come in -
5. Christ, you   lead,   and   we   shall   fol - low,   stum - bling

WORDS and MUSIC: Marty Haugen

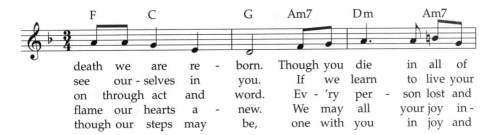

death	we	are	re	-	born.	Though you	die		in	all	of
see	our	- selves	in		you.	If	we	learn	to	live	your
on	through	act	and		word.	Ev	- 'ry	per -	son	lost	and
flame	our	hearts	a	-	new.	We	may	all	your	joy	in -
though	our	steps	may		be,	one	with	you	in	joy	and

his	-	t'ry,	still	you	rise	with	ev	-	'ry
sto	-	ry,	we	may	die	to	rise		a	-
bro	-	ken	wears	the	bod	- y	of		our
her	-	it	if	we	bear	the	cross		with
sor	-	row,	we	the	riv	- er,	you		the

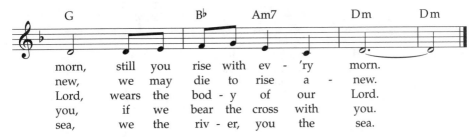

morn,	still	you	rise	with	ev	-	'ry	morn.
new,	we	may	die	to	rise		a	-	new.
Lord,	wears	the	bod	- y	of		our	Lord.
you,	if	we	bear	the	cross		with	you.
sea,	we	the	riv	- er,	you		the	sea.

Lenten Verses:

General: Light of life beyond conceiving, mighty spirit of our Lord,
give new strength to our believing, give us faith to live your word.

1st Sunday: From the dawning of creation, you have loved us as your own.
Stay with us through all temptation, make us turn to you alone.

2nd Sunday: In our call to be a blessing, may we be a blessing true.
May we live and die confessing Christ as Lord of all we do.

3rd Sunday: Living Water of salvation, be the fountain of each soul,
springing up in new creation, flow in us and make us whole.

4th Sunday: Give us eyes to see you clearly, make us children of your light.
Give us hearts to live more nearly as your gospel, shining bright.

5th Sunday: God of all our fear and sorrow, God who lives beyond our death,
hold us close through each tomorrow, love as near as every breath.

135 You Are the One

John 14:6

1. How I love you; you are the one; you are the one! How I love you; you are the one for me!
2. I was so lost, but you showed the way, 'cause you are the way. I was so lost, but you showed the way to me!
3. I was lied to, but you told the truth, 'cause you are the truth. I was lied to, but you showed the truth to me.

4. How I love you; you are the one; you are the one! How I love you; you are the one for me!
5. I was dy - ing, but you gave me life, 'cause you are the life. I was dy - ing, and you gave your life for me!
6. Hal - le - lu - jah! You are the one; you are the one! Hal - le - lu - jah! You are the one for me!

WORDS and MUSIC: Keith and Melody Green

© 1982 Birdwing Music/BMG Songs/Ears to Hear Music

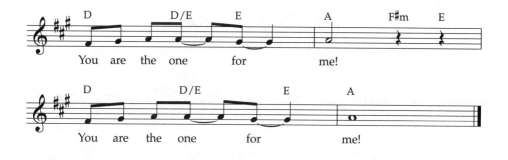

You are the one for me!

You are the one for me!

Psalm 25:4

Show Me Your Ways

136

Show me your ways that I may walk with

you. Show me your ways; I put my hope in

you. The cry of my heart is to love you more, to

live with the touch of your hand, strong-er each

day. Show me your ways.

WORDS and MUSIC: Russell Fragar

137   Gotta Tell Somebody

Psalm 126:2–3

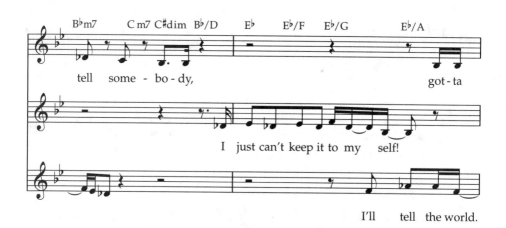

WORDS and MUSIC: William Thomas, Jr.

138   I'm Yours

ev-'ry-thing I am, ev-'ry-thing I'm not. I'm yours, Lord;

try me now and see, see if I can be com-plete-ly yours. 2. You

see if I can be com-plete-ly yours. yours.

2 Corinthians 1:21-22 Take, O Take Me As I Am

139

Take, O take me as I am;

sum - mon out what I shall be;

set your seal up-on my heart and live in me.

WORDS and MUSIC: Iona

140 World Without Walls

Ephesians 2:14

♩=84
CAPO I E♭(D)

E♭(D)

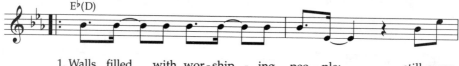

1. Walls filled with wor-ship - ing peo - ple; still some
2. Called by a God of all peo - ple to break

A♭(G)

feel a - lone.
down our walls.

E♭(D)

Walls be - tween cour - te - ous peo - ple have be -
Fol - low a way walked by Je - sus, and the

A♭(G)   B♭(A)

come in - grown.   There are walls un -
bar - ri - er falls.   We'll be free from

A♭(G)(add9)   E♭(D)

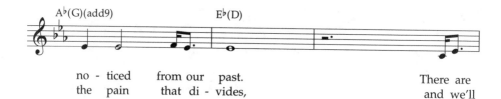

no - ticed from our past.   There are
the pain that di - vides,   and we'll

WORDS and MUSIC: Dan Paul and Steve Fietz

© 1994 Dan Paul

141

My Lord and I
(The Water Is Wide)

MUSIC: Traditional
WORDS: New words and arr: Stephen Reinhardt

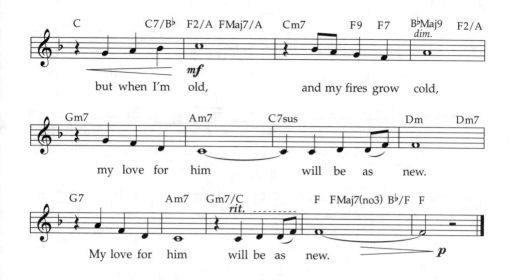

but when I'm old, and my fires grow cold,

my love for him will be as new.

My love for him will be as new.

All My Life

142

My free - dom, my rea - son,

my sav - ior, that's what you are to me.

You free me, com-plete me, my sav - ior, that's what

you are. There's no oth - er like you; there's

WORDS and MUSIC: Libby Huirua,
Wayne Huirua, and Mark DeJong

no one be - side you. You're more than my

heart can con - tain. And I will love you all my life,

for you are my rea - son, the one that I live

for. And I will love you all my life,

for you are my rea - son. You're the

one. And I will one that I live for.

143   **Firm Foundation**   *2 Timothy 2:19*

♩=112 *With confidence*

Je - sus, you're my firm foun - da - tion;

WORDS and MUSIC: Nancy Gordon and Jamie Harvill

144

Your Love

Psalm 139:7–10; Romans 8:35–39

1. Where can I go from your spir-it; how can I es-cape your love?
(2. Where) can I flee from your pres-ence, now that you a-bide in my heart?
(3. Who) can ex-plain your mer-cy; who can com-pre-hend your ways?
(4. I) just want to live in your pres-ence, wor-ship you with all of my heart.

Your love for me is deep-er than the sea and high-er than the heav-ens a-bove.
My heart is your home, your tem-ple, your throne, so what could ev-er keep us a-part?
You showed me your grace by tak-ing my place and wash-ing all my sor-row a-way.
Show me the way, draw me clos-er each day, don't let an-y-thing keep us a-part.

2. Where
4. I

CHORUS

Your love is high-er than the heav-ens; your love is deep-er than the o-cean; noth-ing in cre-a-tion could take

WORDS and MUSIC: Martin J. Nystrom and Don Moen

145   To Love You

Matthew 13:15–16

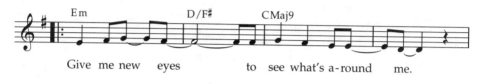

Give me new eyes to see what's a-round me.

Give me new ears to hear what you say.

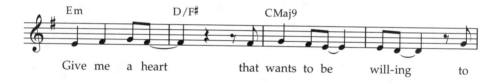

Give me a heart that wants to be will-ing to

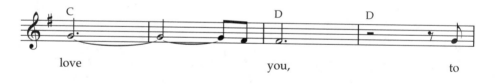

love you, to

love you.

Trust, un - der-stand - ing, cour-age, and hope,

WORDS and MUSIC: Josh Elson and Andra Moran

146

Love Is

1 Corinthians 13

♩=70 *Easy country feel*

If I walk with the Lord all my days, read the good book and follow in his ways, and if I praise his name in ev-'ry-thing I do, but don't have love, I do noth-ing. If I give all I own to the poor and bring ten thou-sand souls to heav-en's door, and if I heal the sick or cause the blind to see, but don't have love, I do noth-ing. Love is pa-tient and kind;

WORDS and MUSIC: Stephen Reinhardt

147 You Live My Love

John 13:34–36

WORDS and MUSIC: Andra Moran and Jennifer Schott

WORDS and MUSIC: Leonard Plick

149   Lula Lulay

Luke 2:15–20

1. Sweet was the song the young girl sang;
2. Sweet were the words the shep-herds prayed;

sweet-er the bells of heav-en rang
sweet-er the gifts of love they gave

as she held him, her new-ly born
as she rocked him and whis-pered his

son.
name.

Gone were the hours of pain and tears,
Gone were the days of Zi - on's tears,

mem - 'ries of all the doubts and fears
mem - 'ries of all the cap - tive years

WORDS and MUSIC: Stephen Reinhardt

lost in the won-der of a new life be - gun.
lost in the won-der of a young girl's re - frain:

CHORUS

Lu - la, lu - la, lu - la, lu - lay.

Sweet was the lull-a - by she sang on that day.

Lu - la, lu - la, lu - la, lu - lay.

Sweet was her song on that day.

Dim. Last time Rall.   *3rd time to Coda*

Lu - la, lu - la, lu - lay.

D.S. al Coda

lay.

CODA

lay.

* *May be sung as an alternate melody for performance.*

150

Lift Me Up

(An Easter Celebration Song)

John 20:22, 29

♩=128 *Joyously*

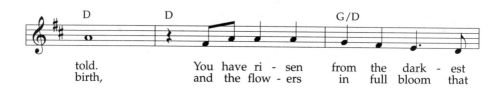

1. You have ris - en   from be - yond,   just   as   you fore -
2. Like the spring - time   of our land   that   ush - ers   in   re -

told.   You have ri - sen   from   the   dark - est
birth,   and the flow - ers   in   full   bloom   that

night - time, oh   so   cold.   I   will nev - er
dress   our moth - er   earth,   you have giv - en

be   a - fraid,   for   you   have shown   me   love.
me   such   hope   in   faith   that   you   dis - played.

D   G/D   C   *top notes are harmony*

Fill - ing me with   ra - diant light, you   lift   me   up   a -
Je - sus, fill   me   with your light, and show   to   me   the

WORDS and MUSIC: William Campbell

151   One Spirit of Love   *1 Corinthians 12:4–28*

♩=90 *Light reggae feel*

1. Ma - ny are the won-ders of God,   ma - ny doors o - pen wide,
2. Some will be the teach-ers of life,   some the preach-ers of love,
3. Liv - ing as the bod - y of Christ   and the heart of the earth

ma - ny roads that are still   un - trav - eled.
some the fath - ers and some   the moth - ers.
and the hands that will break   new ground,

Ma - ny are the gifts that we share;   ma - ny bur-dens we bear,
Some will be the ones who will care;   some will list - en and share,
cel - e-brate the gifts from with-in;   now it's time to be - gin.

ma - ny mys - ter - ies still   un - rav - eled.
serv - ing God while they serve   each oth - er.
God's peo - ple can turn   the world a - round now.

Ma-ny gifts, one spir-it of love,   one spir-it of love.

Ma-ny gifts, one spir - it of love,

one spir-it of love.

One spiri-it of love,   one spir-it of love.

WORDS and MUSIC: Paul B. Svenson

We Are an Offering

153   We Will Not Offer You

Hebrews 13:15–16
Revelation 5:12

♩=ca. 76 *Reggae*

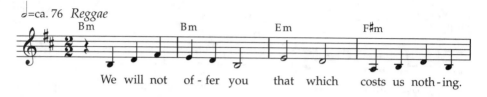

We will not of-fer you that which costs us noth-ing.

We will not give to you the least of what we have.

For you for-gave us and healed us with your suf-f'ring,

and you are wor-thy of the best that we can give.

REFRAIN

So we bring a gift, a sac-ri-fice: the way in which we

live. We bring a gift, a sac-ri-fice, the

of-f'ring that we give. We bring a gift, a

WORDS: Dan Adler; arr. Nylea L. Butler-Moore

154

What Can I Give?

Mark 10:45

You give me life. You give me love. You give me light shin-ing down from a-bove. Oh, what a gift to know the grace of Je-sus Christ. Oh, what a gift to know this grace. You paid the price. You took my place. Oh, what a gift to know this peace. Oh, what a joy. What can I give? How to re-pay the one who gave

WORDS and MUSIC: Scott Tyring

it all a - way? What can I give for such a love, my tri-bute to my God a-bove? Ac-cept this gift; ac-cept my life I give to you.

Walk in the Light

1 John 1:5–7

155

1. & 4. Walk in the light, loved in God's sight,
2. Come take my hand; heal this scarred land; to-
3. We're not a - lone, left on our own.

thru the dark night, walk, walk in the
geth - er we'll stand; come, come take my
Loved as God's own, we're, we're not a -

after last verse

light.
hand.
lone.

(4) Walk in the light.
rit.

WORDS and MUSIC: Jim Strathdee

156 You Are Welcome

1 Corinthians 11:23–26
Matthew 22:1–10

You are wel - come, wel-come to this ho-ly tab - le, yes,

You are wel - come, you are wel-come here.

Verses are in full music edition.

WORDS and MUSIC: O. I. Cricket Harrison

157 Only by Grace

Ephesians 2:8

On-ly by grace can we en - ter; on - ly by grace can we stand;

not by our hu - man en-deav - or,

but by the blood of the Lamb. In - to your pres - ence you call

us. You call us to come

WORDS and MUSIC: Gerrit Gustafson

158 Come to the Table of Mercy

1 Cor. 10:16–17

Come to the ta - ble of mer - cy, pre-
pared with the wine and the bread.

All who are hun - gry and thirst - y,
come and your souls will be fed.

Come at the Lord's in - vi - ta - tion, re-
ceive from his nail - scarred hand.

Eat of the bread of sal - va - tion,
drink of the blood of the Lamb.

WORDS and MUSIC: Claire Cloninger and Martin J. Nystrom

All Are Welcome

All are wel - come, friend and stran-ger, at the ban - quet

of the Sav - ior. All are wel - come. All are wel-come

here.

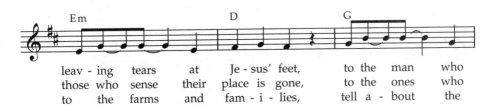

1. From the wo - man who comes cry - ing,
2. From the ones who feel for - got - ten,
3. Go in - to the streets and cit - ies,

leav - ing tears at Je - sus' feet, to the man who
those who sense their place is gone, to the ones who
to the farms and fam - i - lies, tell a - bout the

knows the right way but can - not see.
live in hun - ger, here you be - long.
splen - did ta - ble, God's mer - cy.

WORDS and MUSIC: Hans Peterson and Larry Olson

160 This Is the Place

Luke 15:22–24

This is the place to cel - e - brate! Leave all your
wor - ries be - hind. Let us join hands, for - get the
past. Come share the bread and the wine.

1. We come here with full hearts,
2. This world is a chal - leng - ing place.

joy and sad - ness, an - ger and love.
Hate and hurt feel - ings we'll put a - side.

Let us re - mem - ber the won - der - ful grace
We must hold on - to the pro - mise of hope.

giv - en to all from a - bove.
Let our God be our guide.

WORDS and MUSIC: Andra Moran

Here Is Bread

WORDS and MUSIC: Graham Kendrick

162   Remember Me   *1 Corinthians 11:23–25*

On the night You were be - trayed You took the bread;
night You were be - trayed You held the cup;

af - ter giv - ing thanks, You broke it and
af - ter giv - ing thanks, You lift - ed it

said, "This is My bod - y, bro - ken for
up. "This is My

you, and as you eat it, re - mem - ber

Me. This is My bod - y, bro - ken for

you, and as you eat it, re - mem - ber

Me." On the blood, poured out for

you, and as you drink it, re - mem - ber

WORDS and MUSIC: Gerrit Gustafson
and Martin J. Nystrom

163   Come to the Table of the Lord *Matthew 26:26–28*
Luke 14:21

♩=54 *With energy, in one*

1. Sis - ters and bro - thers, gath - er the oth - ers.
2. Call up the preach-ers, send for the teach-ers.
3. Sis - ters and bro - thers, ga - ther the oth-ers.

Come to the ta - ble of the Lord!
Come to the ta - ble of the Lord!
Come to the ta - ble of the Lord!

Wel - come the cry - ing, the poor, and the dy - ing to
Sum - mon young peo - ple, bring in old peo - ple to
In - vite the nee - dy, beck - on the gree - dy, be

feast at the ban - quet of the Lord.
share in the ban - quet of the
fed at the ta - ble of the

Lord. We re - mem-ber the

words that Je - sus said when he raised the cup and he

blessed the bread: "This bread is my bo - dy, God's

WORDS and MUSIC: Audrey Borschel

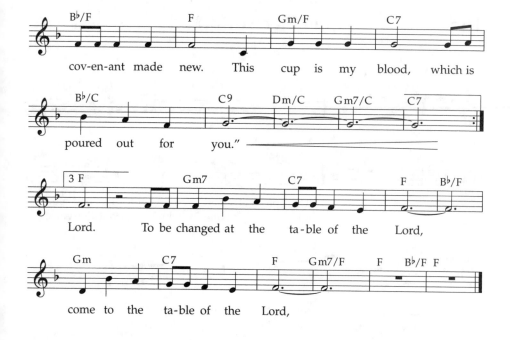

cov-en-ant made new. This cup is my blood, which is

poured out for you." ———————

Lord. To be changed at the ta-ble of the Lord,

come to the ta-ble of the Lord,

1 Corinthians 11:23–26 **We Have Been Redeemed** 164

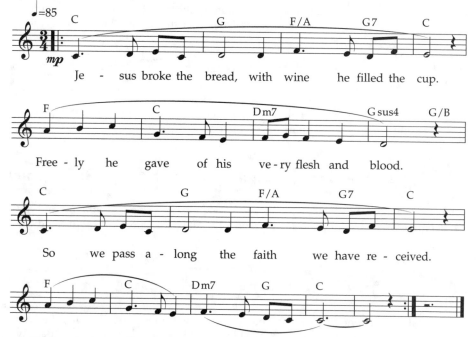

Je - sus broke the bread, with wine he filled the cup.

Free - ly he gave of his ve - ry flesh and blood.

So we pass a - long the faith we have re - ceived.

God's spir-it makes us one; we have been re - deemed.

WORDS and MUSIC: Michael Carlson

165 One Piece of Bread

Matthew 26:26–29

One piece of bread, bless-ing it he said:
One cup of wine flow-ing from the vine,

"Take and eat the por - tion bro - ken for you.
"Take and drink the por - tion shed for your sins,

Come to the Lord, hun - ger nev - er-more." So our
poured out like rain. Nev - er thirst a - gain, share this

souls were fed, one piece of bread.
life of mine," one cup of wine.

One Fa - ther sent his on - ly Son. One Spir-it and the
(2nd time) One Fa - ther sent his on - ly Son. One Spir-it and the

three are one. One bo - dy and he bids us, "Come, be my
three are one. One ta - ble in the wild - er - ness, "Be my

WORDS: Thom Schuyler
MUSIC: Craig Bickhardt

guest, be my guest." One qui - et room
guest, be my guest."

where our hearts com - mune, where our souls are fed,

one piece of bread.

"Come and - re - ceive,

all who will be - lieve. Share this life of mine,

one cup of wine. Let your souls be fed, one piece of

bread."

rit.

166   You Are the Bread

John 6:51

love, feed-ing the world your love,

feed-ing the world your love.

John 6:50–57

Lord, We Need Bread

167

♩=72–78

1. Lord, we need bread that feeds us;
2. Lord, give us bread that feeds us;
3. You are the bread that feeds us;

Lord, we need drink that heals;
Lord, give us drink that heals;
you are the drink that heals;

we need a word that cheers us;
Lord, speak the word that cheers us;
you are the word that cheers us;

we need a life that en - dures.
Lord, grant us life that en - dures.
Lord, you're the life that en - dures.

WORDS: Hartmut Handt
tr: S. T. Kimbrough, Jr.
MUSIC: David Plüss

© 2000 General Board of Global Ministries, GBGMusik

168

Table of Love

Mark 14:22-24

♩=76 *Pop*

1. Here we are, you and me; I won-der if
2. Draw me in as I am; I hope that you

we're s'pposed to be here at this
will un - der - stand as I come to this

ta - ble. of love.
ta - ble

3. I am tired, I am worn, I am bro-
4. I was lost, now I'm found, since we all

ken, I am torn. So I come to this ta - ble.
have gath-ered 'round here at this ta - ble.

I let your peace fill my soul,
I was blind, now I see

WORDS and MUSIC: Andra Moran and Josh Elson   © 2003 AMMO music (ASCAP)/wet cement songs

169   We Remember You   *Revelation 5:12*

1. We re-mem-ber you, we re-mem-ber you; by your sac-ri-fice of love all glo-ry now is due. At this ta-ble here mer-cy hov-ers near.

2. Pre-cious ris-en Lamb, Je-sus who was slain, now en-throned in glo - ry, for-ev-er you will reign. Glad-ly we em-brace both these signs of grace.

Thanks is of-fered up; in this bread and cup we re-mem-ber you.

WORDS and MUSIC: Walt Harrah

♩=75

One body, broken,
words now are spoken, "for you, for you."
One who has suffered, one life he offered for you, for
you. "Forgive them," he said;
broken, he bled, given and shed for you.

We, once divided,
now are united in Christ, in Christ.
God's ancient promise poured out upon us in Christ, in
Christ. Baptized, we're whole, we're
strangers no more. All is restored in Christ.

One body gathered
here to remember in peace, in peace.
One who is able calls to the table in peace, in
peace. "This wine and this bread, a
new covenant. Take and be fed in peace."

WORDS and MUSIC: Jay Beech

© 1994 Augsburg Fortress. Used by permission.

171 Holy Light

Luke 24:13–32

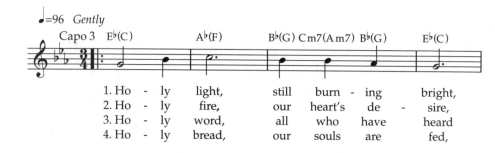

1. Ho - ly light, still burn - ing bright,
2. Ho - ly fire, our heart's de - sire,
3. Ho - ly word, all who have heard
4. Ho - ly bread, our souls are fed,

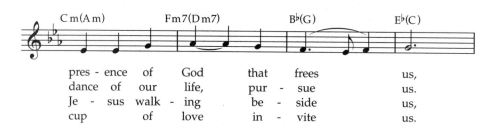

pres - ence of God that frees us,
dance of our life, pur - sue us.
Je - sus walk - ing be - side us,
cup of love in - vite us.

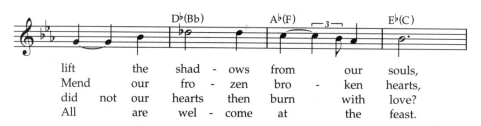

lift the shad - ows from our souls,
Mend our fro - zen bro - ken hearts,
did not our hearts then burn with love?
All are wel - come at the feast.

shine through our lives, Lord Je - sus. sus.
Spir - it of God, re - new us. us.
Word of our God, now guide us. us.
Bread of the world, u - nite us.

us. Bread of the world, u - nite us.

WORDS and MUSIC: Jim Strathdee

Gather Your People

1. Draw us forth to the ta - ble of life:
2. We are parts of the bod - y of Christ,
3. No more harm on the moun - tain of God;
4. Wash us, Lord, in the wa - ters of life,

broth - ers and sis - ters, each of us called to
need - ing each oth - er, each of the gifts the
swords in - to plow - shares. Free us, O Lord, from
wa - ters of mer - cy, wa - ters of hope that

walk in your light.
Spir - it pro - vides.
hard - ness of heart.
flow from your side.

WORDS and MUSIC: Bob Hurd

173 Take Your Place at the Table

1 Cor. 11:23–25

WORDS and MUSIC: Kirk Dearman,
Deby Dearman, and Nancy Gordon

174 One Body in Christ

Ephesians 4:4–6

♩=92

A | A
We come as stran-gers; Christ

E | F♯m | D | A | E
makes us one, drawn by love's ho-ly mys-t'ry.

A | E
Called by the Spir-it to be peo-ple of God, we re-

D | E | 𝄋 A
joice as we start on the jour-ney. So take my hand, come

D | A | Bm | E
walk with me; to-geth-er let us be God's peo-ple,

F♯m | D | Bm — 3 — | E
shar-ing the sto-ries of our lives, no long-er a-lone.
bring-ing the lost and lone-ly ones to find heal-ing here!

A | D | A
For God is here; love lights our way; and we will walk this

E | F♯m — 3 — | A/E E | *To Coda*
road to-ge-ther, one peo-ple of God, one bo-dy in

WORDS and MUSIC: O. I. Cricket Harrison

175   From This Very Place

Acts 13:47

1. From this ver-y place, Lord, touch the na - tions;
2. Melt these hearts of stone with your com-pas - sion;

let us be a light to ev - 'ry race.
let us see oth - ers through eyes of grace.

Hear our hum-ble cry that all would know you as we go
Fill us with the fire of your sweet spir - it as we go

from this ver-y place. 'Til ev-'ry knee bows and
from this ver-y place.

ev - 'ry tongue sings praise, 'til ev-'ry - one hears of your

grace, we will lay down our lives and

pray that your bless - ings flow from this place.

WORDS and MUSIC: Stefan Youngblood; arr: Michael Carlson

place.   We will lay

down our lives and pray that sal-va-tion flows from this place.

Let your heal-ing flow from this place.   Let your

bless-ings flow from this place.

James 2:15–16

Go in Peace

176

♩=135

Go in peace and serve the Lord. Thanks be to God.

Go in peace and serve the Lord. Thanks be to God.

2. Go in joy   3. Go in love

WORDS and MUSIC : Jay Beech

177

Live for Jesus

Matthew 28:19

1, 6. I	will	live	my	life	for	Je - sus;	I	will
2. I	will	seek	the	lost	and	lone - ly;	I	will
3. I	will	teach	the	sa - cred	sto - ries;	I	will
4. I	will	go	and	make	dis - ci - ples;	I	will
5. I	will	feed	them when	they're	hun - gry,	give them

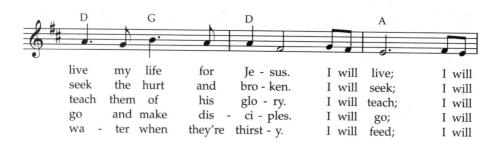

live	my	life	for	Je - sus.	I will live;	I will
seek	the	hurt	and	bro - ken.	I will seek;	I will
teach	them	of	his	glo - ry.	I will teach;	I will
go	and make	dis - ci - ples.	I will go;	I will
wa - ter when	they're	thirst - y.	I will feed;	I will

give.	I will live	my life	for	Je - sus.
seek.	I will live	my life	for	Je - sus.
teach.	I will live	my life	for	Je - sus.
go.	I will live	my life	for	Je - sus.
give.	I will live	my life	for	Je - sus.

Intro, Interlude after verse 3, ending.

WORDS and MUSIC: Steven Staicoff

In the Name of the Lord

I bless you in the name of the Lord; I bless you in the name of the Lord. As we leave this place, I of-fer this grace and bless you in the name of the Lord.

2. I thank you

3. I send you

WORDS and MUSIC: Steven B. Eulberg

179

I Shall Walk

Psalm 116:9

I shall walk* in the pre-sence of God. I shall

walk. With the sun and the rain up - on

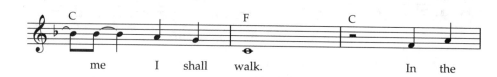

me I shall walk. In the

land of the liv-ing, liv - ing land I shall walk.

With my sis - ters and bro - thers a - round

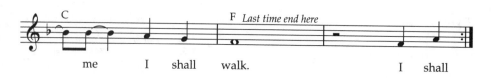

me I shall walk. I shall

* sing, pray, work, love, walk

WORDS and MUSIC: Larry Dittberner

Nurtured by the Spirit

Nur-tured by the Spi - rit, walk-ing in God's light, we are

o - pen to the vi-sion from a - bove. Shar-ing fruits of heav-en,

car - ing for the right, we will walk with the mis - sion of

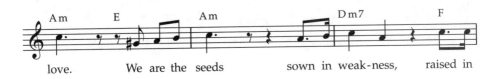

love. We are the seeds sown in weak-ness, raised in

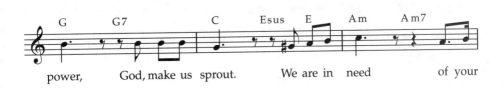

power, God, make us sprout. We are in need of your

Spi - rit; now's the hour: God, send us out! out!

WORDS and MUSIC: Per Harling

181 May You Run and Not Be Weary

Isaiah 40:31

May you run and not be wear-

- y. May your heart be filled with song. And may the

love of God con-tin - ue to give you hope and

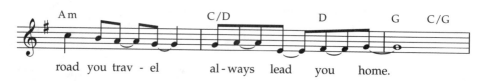

keep you strong. And may you run and not be wear -

- y. May your life be filled with joy. And may the

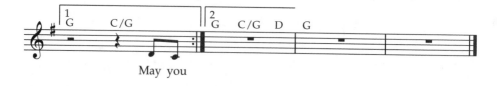

road you trav - el al - ways lead you home.

May you

WORDS and MUSIC: Handt Hanson, and Paul Murakami; arr. Henry Wiens

Wherever You Go

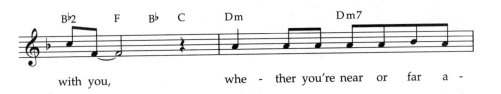

Wher - ev - er you go,   God goes

with you,   whe - ther you're near   or   far   a -

way.   Wher - ev - er   you   walk,   God walks

with you,   bring-ing   strength   and   bless-ing   to   your

day.   Wher - day   .

WORDS and MUSIC: Paul B. Svenson

183

Go in Peace

1 Samuel 20:42

♩=96

Go in peace, go in peace, go in peace, God bless you. May God's grace be with you, friend, both now and when we meet a - gain.

Repeat as desired

WORDS and MUSIC: Andra Moran and Jeff Crow

AMMO music (ASCAP), Song Planet/BNI

Soon and Very Soon

♩=116 *Gospel*

1. Soon and ver - y soon, we are going to see the King;
2. No more dy - ing there, we are going to see the King;
3. No more cry - ing there, we are going to see the King;

soon and ver - y soon, we are going to see the King;
no more dy - ing there, we are going to see the King;
no more cry - ing there, we are going to see the King;

soon and ver - y soon, we are going to see the King.   Hal-le-
no more dy - ing there, we are going to see the King.
no more cry - ing there, we are going to see the King.

lu - jah! Hal-le - lu - jah! We're going to see the King.

185 Go Outside

Where will you go? What will you do?

How will you live what you know is true?

What will you say? How will you grow

when it's time to go? Go

out - side these walls, out - side the lines,

out-side the bound - 'ries and the things that di - vide, out-

WORDS and MUSIC: Jeff Crow and Andra Moran

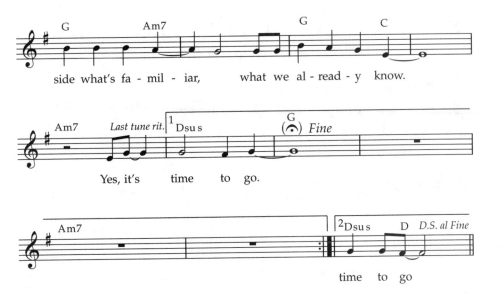

side what's fa - mil - iar, what we al - read - y know.

Am7   *Last tune rit.* 1.Dsus   G ⌢ *Fine*

Yes, it's time to go.

Am7   2.Dsus   D   *D.S. al Fine*

time to go

John 6:35   ## Halleluya! We Sing Your Praises   **186**

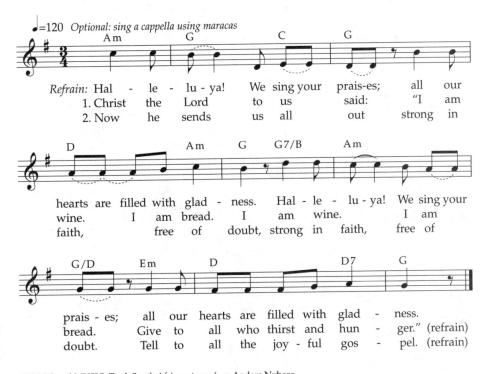

♩=120 *Optional: sing a cappella using maracas*

| Am | G | C | G |

Refrain: Hal - le - lu - ya! We sing your prais-es; all our
1. Christ the Lord to us said: "I am
2. Now he sends us all out strong in

D   Am G G7/B   Am

hearts are filled with glad - ness. Hal - le - lu - ya! We sing your
wine.   I am bread.   I am wine.   I am
faith,   free of doubt, strong in faith,   free of

G/D   Em   D   D7   G

prais - es; all our hearts are filled with glad - ness.
bread.   Give to all who thirst and hun - ger." (refrain)
doubt.   Tell to all the joy - ful gos - pel. (refrain)

WORDS and MUSIC: Trad. South African; trans/arr. Anders Nyberg

187

May the Lord Bless You and Keep You

Numbers 6:24–26

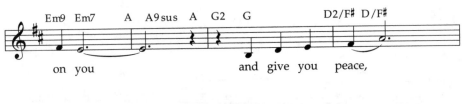

on you   and give you   peace,

and give you   peace   for - ev - er   and   ev - er - more.

Now go   with   God,   go   in   his   care,   and un -

til   we meet a - gain,   we   leave you   with   this   prayer:
(I)

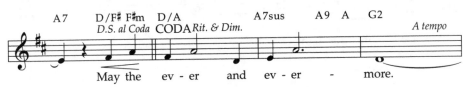

May the   ev - er   and   ev - er   -   more.

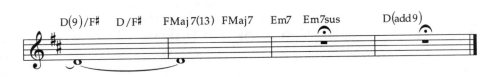

188   Go Out as People of God

Mark 2:1–12

Go out as peo-ple of God. Go out as peo-ple of hope. Go out as peo-ple re - newed. Your sins are for - giv'n; you are made whole; now walk in the light of God.

WORDS and MUSIC: Gloria Lien

189   The Peace of the Earth

John 14:27

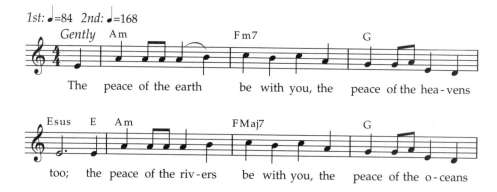

The peace of the earth be with you, the peace of the hea - vens too; the peace of the riv - ers be with you, the peace of the o - ceans

WORDS and MUSIC: Iona

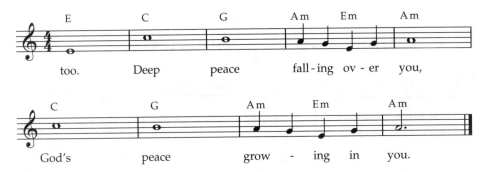

too. Deep peace fall-ing ov-er you,

God's peace grow - ing in you.

Philippians 4:7–9

Peace Be Yours

190

♩=106 *Gently*

1. Peace be yours. May the Lord be with you
2. Peace be yours as you scat - ter from here.

as we gath - er now and your whole life through,
An - y-where you go, God is al - ways near,

bless - ing and mer - cy and whole - ness too.
lov - ing and calm - ing your deep - est fear.

May God's peace be yours.

WORDS and MUSIC: Blair A'Hearn

Index of Copyright Owners

Age to Age Music, Inc.
See The Loving Company

Blair A'Hearn
1511 Spyglass Road
Normal, IL 61761

Almo-Irving Publishing
1904 Adelicia Avenue
Nashville, TN 37212

AMMO music
3801 Richland Avenue
Nashville, TN 37205
www.jandamusic.com

Asian Institute for Liturgy
and Music
P.O. Box 10533
Broadway Centrum
Quezon City 1112
Philippines

Augsburg Fortress
PO Box 1209
Minneapolis, MN 55440
www.augsburgfortress.org

Stephen Austin
P. O. Box 4464
San Diego, CA 92164

Big Baby Music, Inc.
c/o Leonard Plick
2642 Huntington Drive
Duarte, CA 91010

Birdwing Music/
BMG Songs, Inc.
See Music Services

Audrey Borschel
1144 W. 73rd
Indianapolis, IN 46260

Brentwood-Benson Music
Publishing, Inc.
741 Cool Springs Blvd.
Franklin, TN 37067

Bud John Songs, Inc.
Bud John Tunes, Inc.
See Music Services

William Campbell
PO Box 8551
Tucson, AZ 85738

CarlsonArts Ministries
3716 Oil Creek Drive
Indianapolis, IN 46268
www.carlsonarts.com

Carol Joy Music
c/o ICG Alliance Music
PO Box 24149
Nashville, TN 37202

CCCM Music
See The Copyright Company

Changing Church Forum, Inc.
13901 Fairview Dr..
Burnsville, MN 55337
www.changingchurch.org

CMI/HP Publishing
See Word Music Group, Inc.

The Copyright Company
1025 16th Avenue South, #204
Nashville, TN 37212

Cross the Sky Music
37774 Alpha Avenue
Strawberry Point, IA 52076
www.crossthesky.com

Crouch Music
See Music Services

Curious? Music UK
See Music Services

Dad's Songbook Music
12463 Rancho Bernardo Rd., #123
San Diego, CA 92128

Dakota Road Music
PO Box 90344
Sioux Fall, SD 57109
www.dakotaroadmusic.com

Dayspring Music
See Word Music Group, Inc.

Desert Flower Music
PO Box 1476
Carmichael, CA 95609

Larry Dittberner
293 Superior St.
St. Paul, MN 55102
larrydittberner@attbi.com

Doulos Publishing
See The Copyright Company

Ears to Hear Music
See Music Services

Earthsongs
220 NW 29th Street
Corvallis, OR 97330
www.earthsongsmus.com

Ever Devoted Music
See The Copyright Company

Fernwood Street Music (BMI)
c/o Thom Schuyler
104 Oxton Hill Lane
Nashville, TN 37215

Jim Firth
711 Palermo Drive
Santa Barbara, CA 93105

General Board of Global
Ministries, GBG Musik
475 Riverside Drive, Room 350
New York, NY 10115
212-870-3783

GIA Publications, Inc.
7404 S. Mason Avenue
Chicago, IL 60638
www.giamusic.com

Gloria Publishing
c/o Lord of Life
13724 W. Meeker Blvd.
Sun City West, AZ 85375

Hal Leonard Corporation
P. O. Box 13819
Milwaukee, WI 53213
www.halleonard.com

O.I. Cricket Harrison
1817 Carolyn Drive
Lexington, KY 40502

Heart of the City Ministries
c/o Dan Adler
810 South Seventh Street
Minneapolis, MN 55415

Roger Hellwege
34 E. 22nd Street
Edmond, OK 73013

Here to Him Music Group
3117 N. 7th Street
West Monroe, LA 71291

Bret Hesla
2305 S. 25th Avenue
Minneapolis, MN 55406

Hillsongs
See Integrity, Incorporated

Hope Publishing Co.
380 S. Main Place
Carol Stream, IL 60188
www.hopepublishing.com

Index of Sources

Index of Scriptures

Index of Titles

ISBN 978-0-827280-40-3

9 780827 280403